Mississippian Evolution:
A World-System Perspective

Mississippian Evolution:
A World-System Perspective

By Peter N. Peregrine

Monographs in World Archaeology No. 9

PREHISTORY PRESS

Madison Wisconsin

Prehistory Press
7530 Westward Way
Madison, Wisconsin 53717-2009

James A. Knight, Publisher
Carol J. Bracewell, Managing Editor

ISBN 1-881094-00-6
ISSN 1055-2316

Library of Congress Cataloging-in-Publication Data

Peregrine, Peter N. (Peter Neal), 1963-
    Mississippian evolution : a world-system perspective / by Peter N. Peregrine.
        p.   cm. -- (Monographs in world archaeology, ISSN 1055-2316 ; no. 9)
    Includes bibliographical references.
    ISBN 1-881094-00-6
    1. Mississippian cultures. 2. Indians of North America--Economic conditions.
3. Elites (Social Sciences) 4. Ceremonial exchange.
I. Title. II. Series.
E99.M6815P47   1992
303.4'09762--dc20   92-4142

Contents

Illustrations

Tables

Acknowledgements

This book is a revised version of my dissertation (Peregrine 1990) and I must express my gratitude to the many people who had a hand in its development. My dissertation committee, Richard Blanton, Robert Fry, Christian Johannsen and Jack Waddell, and outside reader, Bruce Smith, spent many hours reading and criticizing this work. They provided a sounding board for my ideas that could not have been matched by any other group of scholars. Criss Helmkamp also read sections of this work and offered many useful comments. George Milner provided important information about American Bottom burial data. Linton Freeman offered useful comments about network analysis and ran several of the graph theoretical statistics when my copy of UCINET was acting up. Leonard Lipshitz looked over the graph theoretical analyses and corroborated their rationale. For their help I thank all these scholars. I did not always heed their advice, but I am deeply grateful for their efforts. I hope this work makes them feel their time was well spent.

The research presented here was partially supported through a David Ross Grant from the Purdue Research Foundation. Computer facilities were provided by the Purdue University Computing Center, the Social Research Institute at Purdue University, and by Juniata College.

Finally, I want to thank James Knight and Carol Bracewell at Prehistory Press for their help in getting this work into print.

1

Introduction

My purpose in writing this book is to develop and evaluate a new theory of Mississippian social evolution based on the world-system perspective. I find existing theories of Mississippian social evolution to be problematic, and, as I argue below, new theory needs to be developed. The world-system perspective has never been used to analyze Mississippian social evolution, and appears to me to be a promising framework. As Jane Schneider (1977:20) suggests, the world-system perspective has tremendous potential for theory building in the social sciences because it "establishes a unity of theory between Western and non-Western peoples, the absence of which has long been problematic in unilineal models of change."

I use the term Mississippian to refer to both specialized subsistence economies and forms of social organization that emerged in the riverine areas of the American midcontinent around A.D. 900 (Smith 1978:480). Bruce Smith (1978:486) defines the specialized subsistence economies as involving "maize horticulture and selective utilization of a limited number of wild plants and animals that represented dependable, seasonally abundant energy resources that could be exploited at a relatively low level of energy expenditure." The forms of social organization were hierarchical, and can probably be most readily classified as chiefdoms (Peebles and Kus 1977), although there was apparently great variability in the degree to which power was centralized (Smith 1978:494; DePratter 1983). What is clear, however, is that these societies were stratified, with individuals having differential access to both food resources and exotic goods (Steponaitis 1986:389-90). Mississippian populations also aggregated around large ceremonial centers that contained distinctive flat-topped mounds and were often palisaded (Reed 1977). Any theory of

Mississippian social evolution, then, has to explain the evolution of three elements: (1) social stratification; (2) subsistence economies based on maize horticulture; and (3) concentration of population around large riverine centers.

Contact-Migration Theories of Mississippian Evolution

Some of the earliest theories of Mississippian social evolution centered on the contact of indigenous peoples with outsiders, in virtually every case from Mesoamerica (an exception is Sears 1954). Among the most interesting of these is Joseph Caldwell's (1958:60) idea of Mississippian participation in the "American Oikoumene" where

> The most distinctive cultural elements seem to have spread during the Mesoamerican Formative Stage and spread far beyond the areas which later developed the Classic Stage New World civilizations. It is this American Oikoumene or area of Nuclear civilization to which we shall ascribe the ultimate origin of some of the later developments in the prehistory of eastern North America.

Caldwell (1958:60) does assume that "Nuclear American features were spread throughout the East by agencies which were in large degree indigenous Eastern." James Griffin (1952:361) echoes this idea:

> Almost certainly this is derived from the Mexican area...[although] It does not look as though this was the result of the movement of any large body of individuals into the...eastern United States.

1

As does Albert Spaulding (1955:25):

> [Mississippian origins] suggest the impor-
> tation of ideas to the eastern United States,
> and the pyramidal mounds and the art
> forms...point to Mexico as the source...the
> contact must have been of such a nature as
> to permit the dissemination of ideas
> without extensive movement of material
> objects or people.

In a recent article, Bruce Smith (1984) discussed these "contact-migration" theories at length, tracing both their origins and the reasons for their ultimate rejection. According to Smith (1984:29-30), these theories are no longer utilized because: (1) Mississippian social evolution is too complex to be easily written off to a prime mover such as contact or migration; and (2) Mississippian social evolution took place rapidly and over a broad region, a pattern that fits "in-situ" development theories better. In addition, "contact-migration" theories do not really explain Mississippian social evolution, but simply shift the focus of origin. They leave the problem of explaining the evolution of cultural elements adopted by Mississippian societies for others to address; a sort of theoretical cop-out. Although "contact-migration" theories of cultural change might be appropriate in situations of political dominance (for example Wallerstein 1974a; Frankenstein and Rowlands 1978), they are certainly "not an appropriate general model for all early socio-political change" (Renfrew 1986:6).

In-Situ Theories of Mississippian Evolution

In contrast to these "contact-migration" theories of Mississippian social evolution are numerous theories of "in-situ" evolution (Kelly 1980). Most consider the three major elements of Mississippian social evolution to be linked; that the adoption of maize horticulture brought about social stratification and the aggregation of population around large centers. Richard Ford (1974:405) perhaps put this idea most plainly when he said that "the processes set in motion by expanding corn agriculture and accompanying problems require solutions that could have led to the Mississippian cultures." Ford (1974:407) explained that "accessibility to food production from a large, politically unified territory can counter local disparities and even total loss can be ameliorated from communal stores of crops grown successfully elsewhere." In short, Ford (1977:181) argued that Mississippian social stratification developed in response to uncertainty in agricultural production, with political leaders distributing food from areas of high production to

areas of low production. Similar ideas have been put forward by many other researchers (for example Griffin 1967:189; Peebles and Kus 1977:445; Kelly 1980:220-21; Morse and Morse 1983:202).

Arguing along similar lines, Melvin Fowler (1974:33-34) explained that the basis of Mississippian social evolution

> was in the development of intensive agri-
> culture as a major subsistence base...
> Village farming communities and a demo-
> graphic growth resulted....With the
> growing populations...more elaborate
> systems of community organization and
> socio-political control developed.

Theories for the origin of Mississippian social evolution relying at least in some measure on "demographic stress" have become increasingly common (for example Kelly 1980:220; Griffin 1985:61-63; Muller 1986:177; Steponaitis 1986:389).

Aligned with these "demographic stress" theories for the evolution of Mississippian societies have also been "warfare" theories like Lewis Larson's (1972:391):

> suitable agricultural lands were a critical
> resource in some areas of the southeast
> during the Mississippian period, consti-
> tuting a causal factor and the primary
> objective of the apparently endemic
> warfare in the area at this time...the some-
> what sophisticated defensive constructions
> which surrounded the towns on or adja-
> cent to the contested agricultural lands
> were highly effective deterrents to attack.

According to this theory, the development of centralized villages and strategies for their defense fostered the rise of strong political leaders (Green 1977).

The problem with all these theories of Mississippian social evolution is that the necessary causal connections are poorly supported by archaeological data. Maize had been grown in North America since about A.D. 200 (Smith 1987:2-15), so its introduction cannot alone explain Mississippian social evolution (Griffin 1985:61). And although the Mississippian peoples apparently did rely more on corn than their predecessors, they were certainly not totally committed to corn agriculture (Chmurny 1973). Indeed, Bruce Smith's definition of Mississippian suggests a diversity in food base rather than a dependence on a single crop (also see Ford 1977:180).

Demographic stress theories are also problematic, as there is little evidence for large enough populations to cause "stress" in either the prehistoric (Bender

1985a) or early historic (DePratter 1983) East. Emigration was always available as a means to reduce population density, and demographic stress as an impetus for cultural complexity in general has been shown to be unsupported in a variety of contexts. Indeed Robert Drennan (1987:320), after comparing population density and political complexity in a variety of archaeologically and ethnographically known chiefdoms, tells us

> patterns of population density and regional population do not seem to wax and wane with apparent indicators of the flourishing and decline of social complexity....I do not think that we can simply treat population growth as the cause of the development of complex society.

Warfare theories fare no better. Although there is some evidence that warfare was widespread in the prehistoric East (Larson 1972; Green 1977), it does not appear to be of endemic proportions in all locations where Mississippian societies evolved. And warfare in the historic East was generally conducted for revenge or building of prestige, rather than the conquest of territory (Kinietz 1965; DePratter 1983; also see DeLiette 1934:375-82; Cadillac 1962:22-28; Raudot 1965:196-202).

All of these "in-situ" theories of Mississippian social evolution share the idea that chiefs acted as altruistic managers (see Earle 1987). Chiefly offices are said to develop in order to redistribute resources or organize the populace to solve adaptive problems; chiefs emerge in response to social and environmental pressures. These theories give little weight to the political ambitions of chiefs. The notion that chiefs are motivated by altruism rather than by political desires has recently received criticism on logical grounds (Blanton 1987; also see Patterson 1986:19-20; Shanks and Tilley 1987), and the assumption that underlies it, that chiefs redistribute goods through their polity in order to even out discrepancies (Service 1975) appears to be incorrect (Feinman and Neitzel 1984; Welch 1986, 1991; Earle 1987).

Gary Feinman and Jill Neitzel (1984) provide dramatic evidence against the idea that chiefs are altruistic managers, and particularly against the idea that chiefs always serve to redistribute goods through their societies. They analyzed 63 chiefdom-level societies in the Americas, and came to the firm conclusion that "redistribution is clearly not the central function of leadership in sedentary prestate societies" (Feinman and Neitzel 1984:56). What Feinman and Neitzel (1984:72-77) did find is tremendous variability in the duties performed by political leaders in these

societies, in status differentiation, and the ability of particular leaders to make and carry out decisions. Their study suggests that any theory based on assumed managerial functions performed by political leaders (such as redistribution) which does not demonstrate the presence of those functions, is open to strong criticism.

Steps Towards a New Theory of Mississippian Evolution

Existing theories do not appear to adequately explain Mississippian social evolution, so new theories are needed. To continue looking at "contact-migration" theories seems pointless. Theories that view the evolution of chiefly offices as altruistic management positions to help counter stress are also problematic. A promising way to proceed in developing new theories for the evolution of Mississippian societies may be to consider the growth of chiefly offices from a political standpoint—a view recently put forward by Vincas Steponaitis.

In his review article "Prehistoric Archaeology in the Southeastern United States, 1970-1985," Steponaitis (1986:392) made the critical point that while existing theories of Mississippian social evolution have shown the advantages centralized leadership could have for reducing stress from warfare and the risks from crop failure, "they have not attempted to reconstruct the social and economic strategies by which chiefly offices were formed." Steponaitis (1986:392) suggested that

> Beads, beaded garments, and other valued craft items probably served as tokens in social transactions. Displayed as possessions, these tokens enhanced personal prestige; presented as gifts, they could be used to build alliances and inflict social debts. Exchanges of such items, especially among budding elites, were instruments of political strategy as much as, if not more than, purely economic activities.

The growth of Mississippian social stratification, in this context, lay in an emergent elite's ability to use exchange as an instrument of political strategy. According to Steponaitis (1986:392), the increased reliance on maize did not cause this situation, but certainly fostered it: "the adoption of maize agriculture, while certainly entailing some risks, also provided greater opportunities for accumulating surpluses that could be deployed for social and political purposes."

Considering the political strategies behind the growth of chiefs may be a productive way to develop a new theory for the origin of Mississippian societies.

A theoretical model based on elite use and control of exotic goods for acquiring political power (as suggested by Steponaitis), in conjunction with other factors, seems reasonable for a variety of reasons. First, there is evidence of exchange systems in the eastern United States dating back into the Late Archaic period (Winters 1968; Goad 1978). Second, exchange systems are well documented in ethnographic literature, which should help in analyzing Mississippian exchange. Third, Mississippian exchange goods are clearly documented in the archaeological record, and have been the object of much interest and research by both professional and avocational archaeologists. Finally, there are a number of compelling theoretical frameworks that consider exchange as an important element in social change, perhaps the most influential today being the world-system perspective.

As suggested by Jane Schneider (1977:20), the world-system perspective developed by Immanuel Wallerstein in his seminal work *The Modern World-System* (1974a) and a concurrent article (1974b) has tremendous potential for theory building in the social sciences because it is able to provide a single theoretical framework in which to analyze both Western and non-Western societies. As Schneider (1977:26) explains, the world-system perspective "pushes social science toward an understanding of change in which Western and non-Western, traditional and modern, peoples are subject, if not to similar outcomes, then at least to similar laws."

The World-System Perspective

The phrase "world-system" denotes both a perspective on cultural evolution and several specific theories of cultural evolution. Wallerstein (1974a, 1976) argued that social science was hindered by theory building in the wrong perspective, that being the unilineal or developmentalist perspective. Developmentalists, Wallerstein (1976:344) claimed, agreed to take "individual society as the basic unit of analysis," despite the fact that economic and political reality contradicted this notion. As Wallerstein (1976:345) explained:

> The key difference between a developmentalist and a world-system perspective is the point of departure, the unit of analysis. A developmentalist perspective assumes that the unit within which social action principally occurs is a politico-cultural unit—the state, or nation, or people—and seeks to explain differences between these units, including why their economies are

different. A world-system perspective assumes, by contrast, that social action takes place in an entity within which there is an ongoing division of labour, and seeks to discover *empirically* whether such an entity is or is not unified politically or culturally, asking *theoretically* what are the consequences of the existence or non-existence of such unity.

The entity within which social action takes place is the world-system. The "world" of a world-system is defined by a division of labor, and not by any specific geographic units (for a more detailed discussion of how world-systems are bounded see Chase-Dunn and Hall 1991b). Individual world-systems are more than just the sum of their constituent polities or cultures, but possess properties of their own (Bach 1980:294). These properties, again, are not units, but economic processes:

> If there is one thing which distinguishes a world-system perspective from any other, it is its insistence that the unit of analysis is a *world*-system defined in terms of *economic* processes and links, and not any units defined in terms of judicial, political, cultural, geographical, etc., criteria (Hopkins and Wallerstein 1977:123).

These ideas are perhaps best summed up by Robert Bach (1980:295): "For the world-system perspective, then, the whole consists of singular economic processes which *form* and *reform* the relations that express patterns or structures."

The world-system perspective begins "with the elementary premise that everything is process" (Wallerstein 1982:91) and that "our acting units or agencies can only be thought of as *formed*, and continually reformed, by the relations between them" (Hopkins 1982:149). However, two other premises are also basic to this perspective. The first is geographic (core/periphery) differentiation "according to which particular populations come to play particular roles, their economic, political, and cultural institutions changing to meet the demands of specialization" (Schneider 1977:20). The second is competition between differentiated areas (cores and peripheries). In short, the world-system perspective "hinges on two overlapping processes—one of competition between various geographically localized populations of unequal power; the other of differentiation, division of labor, and interdependence among these same units" (Schneider 1977:20).

World-Systems Theory

Given this world-system perspective, world-systems theory attempts to define the specific economic processes of different types of world-systems (for some examples see the papers in Chase-Dunn and Hall [1991a] and Rowlands, Larson and Kristiansen [1987]). Wallerstein presents some limited theories of world-system process that define three types of world-systems: (1) world-economies; (2) world-empires; and (3) mini-systems. Despite the impact his theories of world-system process have had in sociology and economic history, Wallerstein shows a lack of understanding when it comes to simple non-Western economic systems. They are not included in any of his discussions even though we would expect them to be if, as Wallerstein himself claims, the world-system is the only true unit of analysis for the social sciences (Peregrine 1988, 1989a). The closest Wallerstein comes to a theory of world-system process for non-Western economies is in defining what he calls a "reciprocal-lineage" economy, the processes of which form "mini-systems" (Wallerstein 1976:345-46). The most basic definition of mini-system given by Wallerstein (1974a:390) is "an entity that has within it a complete division of labor and a single cultural framework." This definition relies on the reification of a culture as the boundary of the system, and this is contrary to the world-system perspective itself, which says economic processes, not cultures, define the "world" of a world-system. The mini-system concept is, therefore, terribly flawed, and this leaves a gaping hole in the world-system perspective.

The theory of "pre-capitalist" world-system process developed by Jane Schneider (1977; reprinted in Chase-Dunn and Hall 1991a) is a step towards plugging this gap. In *The Modern World-System*, Wallerstein (1974:41; also 1989:129-37) stated that "staples account for more of men's economic thrusts than luxuries." Schneider (1977:21) countered that idea, complaining that "For many authorities, Wallerstein among them,...luxuries and bulk goods...are implicitly categorized as opposites....I suggest that this dichotomy is a false one that obscures the systemic properties of the luxury trade." Schneider argued that trade in exotic goods is systemic in nature, and can be analyzed with the same world-system perspective Wallerstein reserves for trade in subsistence goods alone (Peregrine 1989b, 1991a). Using China and India as examples, Schneider hypothesized a pre-capitalist world-system, based upon a division of labor in terms of luxury goods consumed by elites to display and maintain status (also see Abu-Lughod 1989).

Richard Blanton and Gary Feinman (1984) used Schneider's theory of pre-capitalist world-systems in a discussion of indigenous Mesoamerican polities (also see Feinman and Nicholas 1991). Quoting Robert Adams, they defended the idea that: "involvement in [luxury] trade can bring in its wake rapid, massive changes in the structure and technological equipment of a society, as well as in associated patterns of motivation, mobility, and leadership," and argued that "for one to comprehend the political economy of the Mesoamerican polities, one must carefully take into consideration the exchange and consumption of preciosities gained from the luxury trade" (Blanton and Feinman 1984:674, 677). They went on to give evidence in support of the idea that "In Mesoamerica, the goal of political expansion was less the conquest and administration of large masses of people than an endeavor designed to regularize or increase the flow of luxury items, or the raw materials required in the manufacture of luxury items" (Blanton and Feinman 1984:677).

While the theory of pre-capitalist world-systems does open the world-system perspective to the study of non-Western societies, it is difficult to apply to Mississippian social evolution because it assumes a market system. However, a theory of world-system process based on the central element of pre-capitalist world-systems (elite control and manipulation of imported preciosities used to display and maintain elite status), which does not assume the existence of markets, has been put forward by Susan Frankenstein and Michael Rowlands (1978). Their theory of "prestige-good" systems shares many elements with Steponaitis's suggestions about elite control of exotic goods during the Mississippian period, and looks like a promising framework for examining Mississippian social evolution.

Prestige-Good Systems

As explained by Frankenstein and Rowlands (1978:75), elites in any social system display and maintain their status through the control of exotic goods and esoteric knowledge (also see Helms 1979, 1988; Clark 1986). In a prestige-good system these elite symbols are needed by all members of the society for social reproduction (Ekholm 1972, 1977; Friedman and Rowlands 1977; Friedman 1982). Exotic goods may be used to pay social debts, such as bridewealth payments. Esoteric knowledge may be needed to perform rituals of initiation and regeneration. When elites are able to control access to these symbols and knowledge, elite power grows in direct proportion to the growth of the prestige-good system. Frankenstein and Rowlands (1978:76) describe the growth of elite power in this way:

The specific economic characteristics of a prestige-good system are dominated by the political advantage gained through exercising control over access to resources that can only be obtained through external trade...Groups are linked to each other through the competitive exchange of wealth objects as gifts and feasting in continuous cycles of status rivalry. Descent groups reproduce themselves in opposition to each other as their leaders compete for dominance through differential access to resources and labour power.

One element of the world-system perspective, competition between localized polities, is, therefore, inherent in prestige-good systems. The second element, core/periphery differentiation and division of labor, is inherent in the nature of the prestige-goods themselves. By definition, prestige-goods must be exotic or of high labor investment. They embody esoteric knowledge about the world outside the local group or knowledge of special manufacturing techniques (Helms 1988). Because prestige-goods are traded from outside the group or commissioned from artisans with special skills, there is an inherent division of labor in prestige-good systems. Prestige-good systems, then, are another arena of world-system process (with "world," again, being defined by a division of labor and not by any formal geographic units).

The theory I develop and test in the remainder of this book is that the patterns defined earlier as characterizing Mississippian societies (social stratification, the growth of ceremonial centers with large populations, and specialized subsistence economies focused on maize horticulture) evolved in the framework of a prestige-good system.

Prestige-Good Systems and Mississippian Evolution

A basic assumption I make in developing this theory of Mississippian social evolution is that the Mississippian prestige-good system and the emergence of social stratification were elements of the same process, and that both were rooted in and legitimated through the existing social structures of Late Woodland and earlier societies. Prestige-good systems are both social and economic structures: they are economic because they are based on trade; they are social because the control of trade in prestige-goods which forms the basis of political power is legitimated through the existing social structure.

In Chapter 2 I argue that prestige-good systems are based on corporate lineages, and that power is legiti-

mated through existing elder/younger relationships. These relationships are reproduced in the social stratification that emerges as prestige-good systems evolve towards greater political centralization. Elites are social "elders" in prestige-good systems, and are at the top of the political hierarchy, just as elders are in corporate lineages. Commoners are social "juveniles" in prestige-good systems and, as in corporate lineages, serve the elders and accept their political superiority in order to move themselves up the ladder of social maturity.

The argument I make in this work is that Mississippian social stratification evolved out of, and was based in, an existing corporate lineage structure. I argue that lineage elders, who controlled the status symbols and esoteric knowledge of the lineage, fostered the use of these goods and knowledge in ceremonies of social reproduction (as suggested by Steponaitis). As the goods and knowledge came to be in greater demand, the lineage elder's power grew in direct proportion. Certainly fostered by population growth during the Late Woodland period (Morse and Morse 1983; Muller 1986), increasing the demand for prestige-goods and esoteric knowledge, lineage elders during the formative Mississippian period gained enough power to differentiate themselves from other lineage members, and became an emergent elite.

In considering the emergence of social stratification, one must also consider the intensification of production necessary to sustain elites. Indeed, as Colin Renfrew (1982:265) has explained, "all development towards more complex society implies intensification, permitting the support of administrative and other central activities." Intensification for the support of elites is accomplished by either (1) increasing labor inputs, or (2) improving technology (Renfrew 1982:268-75). The technology used for intensification by the Mississippians, maize horticulture and the bow and arrow, were available in the prehistoric East since at least Middle Woodland times. The introduction of these technologies alone, therefore, cannot account for intensified production (Griffin 1985:61). Although maize horticulture and the bow and arrow certainly played a part in intensifying production, they were not the cause. The intensification of production necessary to support Mississippian social stratification must have rested largely on increased labor inputs.

In order to explain Mississippian social evolution through the processes of a prestige-good system, one must therefore explain why individuals would have increased labor to intensify production for the support of elites. The assumption I make follows Renfrew (1982:269) in that "The number of hours a man will work are governed by his perceptions of what he needs to fulfill social and exchange obligations, and to maintain what he considers an adequate standard of living." In this sense, an individual will increase production if he perceives that the increase is necessary to fulfill social obligations and maintain an adequate standard of living. In a prestige-good system, intensification to support elites is necessary, for elites control the prestige-goods needed to fulfill social obligations and to maintain an adequate standard of living. The idea that a prestige-good system was in operation during the Mississippian period suggests that individuals would have intensified production to support their elites in competitive exchanges with others so that they would have had more access to prestige-goods, and hence a better opportunity to socially reproduce themselves at acceptable levels.

As elites compete for exotic goods in a prestige-good system, elites located at nodal points on trade routes, and who have a supportive population, will be able to control those routes and the goods flowing from them. Elites less fortunately located will grow dependent on elites controlling trade routes, and may be undermined by them. Population will be attracted to elites who offer greater access to prestige-goods, and hence better opportunities to socially reproduce in the prestige-good system. In this way Mississippian centers with dense populations could have readily emerged in the central riverine valleys of the midcontinent, where riverine trade could be controlled, and where intensified production was possible.

The concept of Mississippian social evolution based on the processes of a prestige-good system seems to avoid some of the problems present in existing theories. Chiefs emerge because of their ability to control prestige-goods, and perhaps from personal ambition, but not from some desire or need to altruistically manage their society. Social evolution grows out of the systemic interaction of independent polities within the prestige-good system, not from simple migration or diffusion. Maize horticulture and increased subsistence production are not "prime mover" forces behind social evolution, but emerge out of the evolutionary process itself. In short, the theory that Mississippian social evolution derived from the processes of a prestige-good system appears to be less problematic and more explanatory than existing theories.

Plan of the Work

In the next chapter, "Prestige-Good Systems," I consider three prestige-good systems in order to describe their basic social structures. In Chapter 3, "Social Evolution in Prestige-Good Systems," I consider change in three prestige-good systems, and develop and evaluate a theory of change in political power based upon the density of prestige-goods in the system. In Chapter 4, "Prestige-Goods," I analyze prestige objects from societies around the world to develop a definition of prestige-goods, and I examine the use of different types of prestige-goods by systems of differing political complexity. Chapter 5, "The Mississippian Prestige-Good System," contains three hypotheses concerning the distribution of prestige-goods in prestige-good systems. I evaluate these hypotheses to determine if a prestige-good system could have been in operation during the Mississippian period. Chapter 6, "Social Evolution in the Mississippian Prestige-Good System," contains two hypotheses about trade and control of prestige-goods. I evaluate these to determine if a prestige-good system influenced Mississippian societies as they evolved. Finally, in Chapter 7, I apply the theory of political change in prestige-good systems developed in Chapter 3 to the archaeological record of eastern North America, in an attempt to understand Mississippian social evolution through the processes of a prestige-good system. I offer conclusions on the existence of a Mississippian prestige-good system, its importance in understanding Mississippian social evolution, and the utility of world-systems theory for understanding cultural evolution in eastern North America.

2

Prestige-Good Systems

In this chapter I examine a number of existing or ethnographically known prestige-good systems. As I explained in the previous chapter, political power in prestige-good systems rests on the control of exotic goods and esoteric knowledge. The most basic structure of prestige-good systems is that exotic goods are needed by everyone in order to pay for activities necessary to social reproduction, such as bride price, fines, and initiation ceremonies. This analysis of extant prestige-good systems will highlight other structures present in prestige-good systems, and give a fuller picture of these systems and how they operate.

Power and Prestige-Goods

The concept of political power being derived from the control of prestige-goods needed for social reproduction was first considered by Claude Meillassoux (1978) in his essay "'The Economy' in Agricultural Self-sustaining Societies: A Preliminary Analysis." Here Meillassoux develops a theory to explain the control senior lineage members have over junior members in African "self-sustaining" economies. Meillassoux argues that the power of senior lineage members rests on their control of esoteric knowledge and, through bridewealth payments, of nubile women.

Individuals gain esoteric knowledge in these societies as they move through the ranks of society or ally themselves with persons who can pass on such knowledge. In either case, individuals previously initiated or having special knowledge maintain power over the uninitiated or unknowing, for they can choose to either make their special knowledge available or not. As Meillassoux (1978:138-39) explains:

In order to perpetuate their authority, the seniors must extend their knowledge beyond fundamental subsistence skills to new fields (social learning, knowledge of customs, genealogies, history, the rules governing marriage) and even further to artificial fields (magic, divination, religious rituals, etc.). They will try to make this knowledge their exclusive province by setting up barriers to regulate its transmission: institutional barriers like initiation which in its most elaborate forms defines the individual's rank until a very advanced age; and esoteric barriers which are placed around magical, ritual (or medicinal) information so that it is only transmitted to chosen individuals...it is relatively easy for...[a young man] to acquire the vital knowledge necessary for his labour and to occupy a vacant area of land. However the fulfillment of these conditions only provide him with a solitary independence; they do not enable him to achieve a position of authority within his group.

Authority within such a group grows through a young man's recreating, to his advantage, the social world from which he came (Meillassoux 1978:139). He does this by continuing the social norm: he is initiated into ritual societies, he gains special knowledge, he, in short, bows to the elder's power in order to gain the knowledge he needs to become powerful himself.

Control over nubile women, according to Meillassoux (1978:139), is a more important means of gaining power for elder men. He tells us "it is logical in an economy in which the product of labour can

9

only be controlled through the direct control over the producer, to control also—and maybe even more so—the *producer of the producer*, i.e. the procreative woman." By controlling procreative women, elders in African "self-sustaining" societies in essence control the means of production—the very basis of power in Meillassoux's Marxist perspective. Control over nubile women is gained by senior men through the institution of marriage payments made with objects "whose handling is associated with the rank of the person handling them," in short, prestige-goods (Meillassoux 1978:141). Since junior men are not of sufficient rank to acquire the prestige-goods needed for marriage payments, they cannot acquire a wife without the help of a senior male. Again, this gives the senior men power over junior men's ability to reproduce, and in essence, gives them control over the means of production in these African societies.

Elder Power in the Kongo Kingdom

In her book *Power and Prestige: The Rise and Fall of the Kongo Kingdom*, Kajsa Ekholm (1972) takes Meillassoux's perspective and applies it to the analysis of political power in the Kongo kingdom. Ekholm wanted to understand why the king's power rapidly declined following the arrival of Europeans. In doing so she provides a detailed description and analysis of a prestige-good system in operation (I rely on Ekholm here because she presents the Kongo kingdom as a prestige-good system in a lucid and comprehensive manner, but I direct interested readers to Hilton's [1985] and Vansina's [1966] excellent works on the Kongo kingdom for additional information and perspectives on its history that sometimes contrast with Ekholm's).

The Kongo kingdom was located on the African coast south of the Congo delta. The estimated population of this region at the time of contact is between two and three million (Ekholm 1972:11). The population was mainly spread out across Kongo territory, surrounding slash-and-burn agricultural fields, but there also existed capital "cities" with populations up to 100,000 (Ekholm 1972:11-12). The kingdom had six recognized provinces, each with its own capital and provincial ruler, and numerous district and village chiefs (Ekholm 1972:12-13).

The Kongo king had authority over the kingdom's politics, economics, judiciary, and religion (Ekholm 1972:15). Political authority rested on the fact that the kingdom functioned as a single political unit, with the king as its head (Ekholm 1972:16). The king also maintained a personal army "which he sent out to the vassals to enforce payment of tribute, and/or kill the

rebel who refused" (Ekholm 1972:17), which reinforced his political power. This ability to extract tribute shows one aspect of the king's economic authority, but a second was the control he maintained over foreign trade (Ekholm 1972:19-20). Judicial authority derived from the fact that the king was the "supreme court" in the Kongo—disputes that could not otherwise be settled came to him, as well as disputes between provincial chiefs (Ekholm 1972:18-19). Finally, the king's religious authority derived simply from the fact that he was considered "divine" (Ekholm 1972:23-24).

Existing under the king, and subservient to him, were six provincial chiefs. Each had king-like authority in their own provinces, but had to follow delegated orders from the king (Ekholm 1972:25). The king, indeed, appointed these provincial chiefs (Ekholm 1972:26). Below the provincial chiefs were district chiefs, and below them village chiefs, each subservient to those above them in the hierarchy (Ekholm 1972:25). As Ekholm (1972:25) tells us: "the fundamental structure of the Kongo kingdom...was *nothing but a hierarchy of political chiefs.*"

At the local, village level, the Kongo kingdom was organized around landowning matrilineages (Ekholm 1972:30). As described by Jan Vansina (quoted in Ekholm 1972:31):

> The basic unit of the political structure was the village, and the core of every village seems to have been a localized matrilineage. The children of its head would gather there as well as the client lineages....The headmanships of the villages seem to have been hereditary in the core lineages.

Within lineages there was a strict division between the younger generation and the older (Ekholm 1972:36,108). The younger generation was completely subservient to the older, and were continually doing work for them (Ekholm 1972:37,109). However, for a young Kongo man:

> the older he became—with the accompanying rise in status through initiations, marriage, children, etc.—the more his situation improved....But it was not only biological age which was decisive here...the factor which lay behind it was *social age.* Older men could easily find themselves in a lifelong subordinate position because they failed to develop socially....The oldest, biologically, could totally lack any power or influence, but he who had power was always "eldest," socially (Ekholm 1972:37-38).

The fundamental structure of the Kongo kingdom did not differ much from that of a localized matrilineage, it simply existed on a variety of levels. As one moves up the hierarchy of chiefly levels in Kongan society, one can think of oneself simply increasing the scale of a single matrilineage (see Figure 2.1). Indeed "The Kongolese themselves described their society as though it were a single clan" (Ekholm 1972:32). Ekholm (1972:40-41) stresses this point:

In the ethnographic material covering Kongo the 'matrilineage' is especially stressed and in this case all the groupings are depicted by the Kongolese themselves as one single matrilineage, a unit of the same type as the basic unit...the term *kanda* is often used for the minor matrilineages, the matrilineage in its full sense, or for the society as a whole....(1972:40-41).

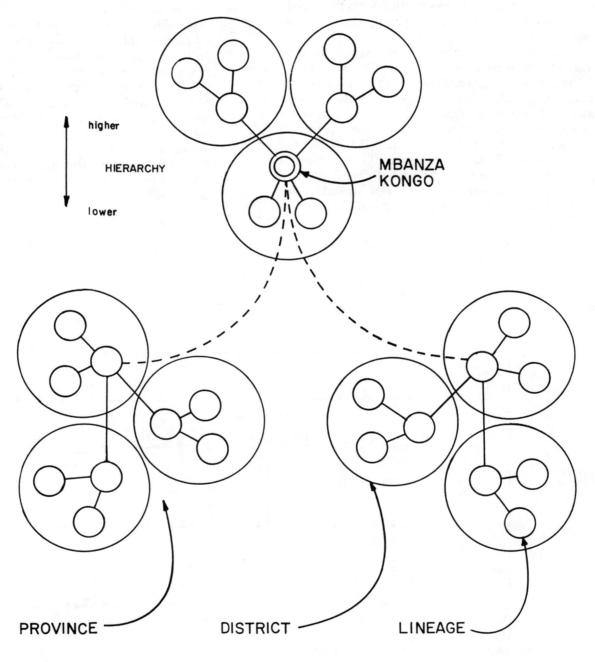

PNP

Figure 2.1. The geo-political structure of the Kongo kingdom (after Ekholm 1972:58).

In essence, the Kongo kingdom was built from the basic element of the localized matrilineage, joined through a political network that mimicked the structural form of the matrilineage (Ekholm 1972:42). Of course, Kongo society was not a single matrilineage, the simple rules of matrilineal exogamy would have prevented its functioning very long (Ekholm 1972:49), but it was a political network of matrilineages. The political structure of this network was very similar to the internal structure of the matrilineages themselves, particularly in terms of elder/younger relations (see Figure 2.2).

These elder/younger relationships within the political network were expressed in patrilineal terms, i.e. father/son and grandfather/grandson (Ekholm 1972:50). In other words, the elder male/younger male differentiation present within matrilineages was reproduced in the political network, using patrilineal terms. Ekholm (1972:51) explains that "What the patrilineal names primarily express is the difference in generations." Just as in the matrilineage, political power in the Kongo kingdom was equitable with social age, and social age was demonstrated, as

Meillassoux suggests, through the control of esoteric knowledge and associated symbols.

In Kongo it was not simply political power, but exotic goods and esoteric knowledge that passed down the chiefly hierarchy, and gave chiefs their position and power. Ekholm (1972:55) makes this point clear:

> [It was] the power of the gods which was delegated from chief to chief, with the help of rites and religious symbols....Through delegation of power, i.e. the transfer of the religious symbols of power, the different political chiefs—the king, the provincial governors, district chiefs, and even village chiefs—took up their patrilineally defined positions within the hierarchy. The king was at the top, and was *tata* [elder] to the subordinate provincial chiefs who were his *muana* [younger]. The provincial chiefs on the other hand held the position of *tata* in relation to the district chiefs, and so on down the line.

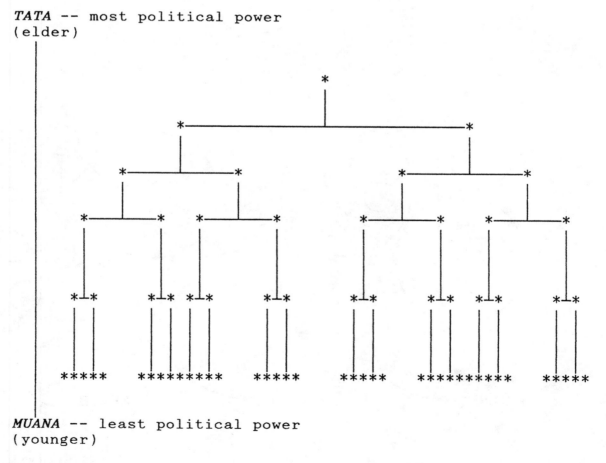

Figure 2.2. Elder/younger hierarchy of the Kongo kingdom (after Ekholm 1972:57). This is the basic structure of all political units, and can be used to show relationships within lineages, districts, or provinces.

Although political chiefs, even the king, were "elected" by other chiefs (or appointed by the king), they were almost universally the socially "eldest" within their matrilineages (Ekholm 1972:56). The reason was simple: between the time of appointment and his crowing, a chief-to-be was expected to gather a considerable amount of riches, in order to, in essence, "buy" his office (Ekholm 1972:56,115). Only matrilineal elders, who controlled a matrilineage's wealth (Ekholm 1972:109), had any hope of amassing the goods to buy their office, and so the power structure of the matrilineage was again reproduced in the political structure of the kingdom.

One can readily see the ramifications of this political structure considered in the light of Meillassoux's ideas about the nature of power in African "self-sustaining" economies. According to Meillassoux, power is held by elders through the control of esoteric knowledge and exotic goods needed to "purchase" nubile women. In the Kongan political hierarchy, power was held by social "elders" though their control of esoteric knowledge and associated symbols. Even the control of nubile women was expressed in the political network of the Kongo kingdom, for Ekholm (1972:61) tells us that

> Marriage in the Kongo society should take place between members of two different "generations", i.e. between the superordinate Tata-group and the subordinate Muana-group...generation was not only a biological category—political relationships were expressed in terms of the different generations and marriage within the same generation was consequently thought of as marriage within one's own group.

Political Power and Prestige-Goods

Political power in the Kongo kingdom rested on the same base as power within localized matrilineages—on the control of esoteric knowledge and associated symbols. More specifically, however, the king's power in Kongo was based upon his control of external trade and the exotic goods coming from it. The king neither controlled land in Kongo, nor had direct coercive power over the people. That type of authority was maintained within the localized matrilineage (Ekholm 1972:83-84). The king only maintained coercive control over his provincial chiefs, just as they maintained coercive control over their direct subordinates in the hierarchy, and so on down the line. As Ekholm (1972:86) describes:

> The relationship between village and the superordinate matrilineage in the district

capital was a relationship *between chiefs*. A superordinate chief's authority was limited, to a large extent, to dealings with his subordinate colleague, the point being that, in principle, he had no possibility of exercising any direct power over the subordinate chief's subjects (Ekholm 1972:86).

As I have shown, within the matrilineages, elders maintained coercive power over the younger generation through their control of esoteric knowledge and associated symbols (Ekholm 1972:111). This same relationship existed between superordinate and subordinate chiefs, who, as I have also shown, shared an elder generation/younger generation relationship themselves. The Kongan king, socially elder to his provincial chiefs, controlled their access to esoteric knowledge and associated symbols. The provincial chiefs, in turn, controlled the access of subordinate chiefs to the knowledge and symbols they had received from the king, and so on down the line until one reaches the matrilineal level of elder control described by Meillassoux.

Ekholm (1972:100-101) offers a clear picture of the political power structure based on the control of prestige-goods, which symbolized social status in Kongan society. She explains that chiefly power

> was based on the fact that they *controlled certain important products in the society*. They did not control land or any other means of production—instead they had control over goods which are usually called prestige objects, products which were not needed for actual material support of life, but were definitely needed for social and political position within the society. Everyone needed them some time or other in order to acquire a wife, pay a fine, initiation fee or membership in an age-set, or to pay for one grade or other in a "secret society", etc. There is nothing strange in the fact that a chief gave away his prestige articles, since it was his subjects' very need of them which motivated his control over them.

This relationship existed between elder and younger members of local matrilineages as well:

> Mother's brother's power over his sister's son was based on control of *prestige articles*. When we say that the lineage chief "managed" over the "commonly owned" property we are of course paraphrasing. Sister's son did not need prestige articles for his material livelihood, but he did need

them on a number of different occasions pertaining to his social career: at puberty rites, marriages, in payment for religious and medical expertise, and for fines, etc. Since the prestige articles were "owned in common" and "managed" by the lineage chiefs, persons lacking property of their own were directly under the chief's power and authority. One could not be deprived of free access to the "means of production" but the means by which one reached full-fledged social membership was another matter (Ekholm 1972:111).

Political Power and Foreign Trade

External trade, for the Kongan king, was with the kings of the surrounding kingdoms. Within Kongo, provincial governors and others were not free to trade with foreigners, but only with their superordinates (Ekholm 1972:128). Trade within Kongo occurred between the generational levels, and not between Kongans and foreigners (Ekholm 1972:129). Ekholm (1972:133) describes this system at length:

> The kings traded for foreign prestige articles, those which were not produced by the native population. This is the crux of the matter: by holding a monopoly on external trade the central power had control of foreign products, a control which was much more effective than trying to keep watch on domestic prestige articles....Kongo's eastern neighbors did not 'need' Kongo's shells—they had their own prestige articles; still they imported shells and used them....The driving force behind this external trade, and thereby the political development, was the need of trade partners to whom chiefs could transmit domestic prestige articles in return for products which the local vassals could not acquire other than through the king. Foreign products were best since they could most effectively be regulated and they need not have any practical use themselves—one could produce the demand for them, even make them indispensable. This occurred when an imported article was raised to the status of a means of payment, perhaps even the most important means of payment.

With the coming of Europeans, the Kongan king's control of prestige-goods obtained from foreign trade eroded, and his power rapidly declined. This occurred partially because many European goods were easily

substituted for Kongan prestige-goods: cotton cloth for raffia cloth, glass beads for shell beads, and the like (Ekholm 1972:103-107). Indeed, Ekholm (1972:106) states that "Those red, white and blue glass beads corresponded to a certain type of shell...which for Kongo's king and his neighbors was 'more valuable than gold and silver'." Equally important was the fact that trade between kings was redirected to European sources, "so that each and every king traded with Europe instead of, as before, with each other" (Ekholm 1972:131). More important, however, was European failure to respect the king's control over foreign trade (Ekholm 1972:102). As Ekholm (1972:138) explains:

> when the Europeans established trade relations directly with the local chiefs, the political network was broken and with it the superordinate position of the central power. The subordinate chiefs then had the possibility of acquiring prestige articles from other channels, and immediately gave up their loyalty and obedience to the king in Mbanza Kongo, launching their own independent careers.

The kings of the African savanna attempted to foil these upstarts in many ways. In particular, they refused to accept European goods to pay social debts, accepting only traditional prestige-goods (Ekholm 1972:114). They also tried to explain to the Europeans what their trading with subordinate chiefs would do: "You see the Mbumu. It is great because all other rivers run into it. It is the same with my chiefs. If they no longer need my gifts they would no longer come to me and I would no longer be anything" (Ekholm 1972:101). The king of Kongo expressed similar ideas in a letter to the Portuguese government (Ekholm 1972:101). Even though the Portuguese agreed, merchants established direct trade with local chiefs, who "built up enough strength to the point where it was possible for them to compete with the traditional authority" (Ekholm 1972:102), and the king's power rapidly declined. This transformation is clearly described by Ekholm (1972:144):

> The arrival of Europeans gave every local chief career possibilities otherwise not available under the traditional system. Earlier the path to power and glory often went via a vassal relationship with one of the larger political power centers, but afterwards, in principle, anyone with ambition and military strength could compete with the traditional authority over the local hegemony.

The Kongo kingdom represents a classic example of a prestige-good system. Superior's control over their subordinate's access to prestige-goods was the basis of political power, legitimated through a framework of elder/younger relations. When prestige-goods became accessible to anyone with the ambition to get them, the superior's power declined. Similarly, for the brief period that superiors were able to maintain control over new, and highly desirable, European-introduced prestige-goods, their power grew (Ekholm 1972:135-136).

However, the Kongan prestige-good system is on an enormous scale, and is highly complex. It may be one of the more extreme examples of a prestige-good system. Jonathan Friedman (1982:186) has suggested that "West Polynesia represents a classic example of the full-blown prestige-goods systems," and it is to that world area that I now turn. Friedman also suggested that the Tongan "empire" is a good example of a western Polynesia prestige-good system. Tonga has an advantage over other systems in that it has been the subject of two primary ethnographies (Mariner 1817 and Gifford 1929), and numerous follow-up and problem-oriented studies (for example Kaeppler 1971a, 1971b; Rutherford 1977; Ferdon 1987). Tonga also represents a prestige-good system very similar to the Kongan example, but on a much smaller scale.

The Tongan Chiefdom

The Tongan archipelago is located in the Pacific Ocean some 2000 miles east of Australia and 600 miles southeast of Fiji. It consists of about 160 islands strung out over 200 miles on a roughly northeast-southwest axis (Kirch 1984:217). Only three islands are of any size: Tongatabu (100 square miles); Haapai (20 square miles); and Vavau (46 square miles). The population in the 1920's was about 25,000, most of whom lived on the three large islands of the archipelago (Gifford 1929:4). Obviously, population was quite dense on these islands (Goldman [1970:281] estimates 150 persons per square mile), and most of the land area was given over to fields and stands of yam, taro, sweet potato, breadfruit, plantains, and coconuts (Goldman 1970:281). This high population was not a recent phenomenon; 150 years earlier Captain Cook reported that most of Tongatabu was in cultivation, and had a very high population (Gifford 1929:5- 7).

Tonga had a dual political structure, with two major leaders: the *Tui Tonga*, who was considered divine, and was the link between humans and deities; and the *Tui Kanokupolu (hau)*, who answered only to the Tui Tonga, and was responsible for secular concerns in the chiefdom (see Figure 2.3; also Kirch 1984:224-25). As described by Basil Thompson (quoted in Kirch 1984:225):

> [the spiritual king]—the Tui Tonga—was lord of the soil, and enjoyed divine honours in virtue of his immortal origin....The temporal king—the Tui Kanokubolu—was the irresponsible sovereign of the people, wielding absolute power of life and death over his subjects, and was charged with the burden of the civil government and the ordering of the tribute due to the gods and their earthly representative, the Tui Tonga.

Both the Tui Tonga and the Tui Kanokupolu had a group of four chiefs and attendants who were known as *falefa*, and served as the Tui's courtiers (Kirch 1984:230-31). Subservient to the Tui Kanokupolu's falefa were a number of local, landholding chiefs, or *eiki*, their attendants, or *matapule*. Subservient to the landholding chiefs were lesser chiefs, also called matapule, hereditary titled craftsmen, or *tohunga*, and finally commoners, or *tua* (Kirch 1984:231-32).

Irving Goldman (1970:314-15) offers an interesting outline of the Tongan political structure through what he describes as four segments of political hierarchy. The first segment refers to the Tui Tonga and Tui Kanokupolu, who maintain ultimate power in Tonga. The second segment refers to the chiefs of landholding lineages, who "were in virtually all respects sovereign in their own jurisdiction. Each major lineage was a replica of the entire administration" (Goldman 1970:315). The third segment refers to subchiefs of the major landholding lineages, "and for its most part a replica in most respects of the major branch, dependent on the major as the major was on the Tui Tonga or his representatives" (Goldman 1970:315). Finally, the fourth segment refers to the patrilocal household (see Figure 2.3). Goldman (1970:315) tells us that "A hierarchy of successive dependencies was the ancient Tongan scheme," and at the base was the patrilocal household.

The organization of these patrilocal households was reproduced in the political hierarchy of Tonga, just as the matrilocal lineages were reproduced in the hierarchy of Kongo. Generation and sex were the basis of rank within the family, and rank was the basis of political power: "The first-born son took the title, the social position, and the leadership in the family" (Goldman 1970:289). Although sisters outranked brothers in formal honor, females did not hold political office or power in Tonga. As explained by Goldman (1970:290):

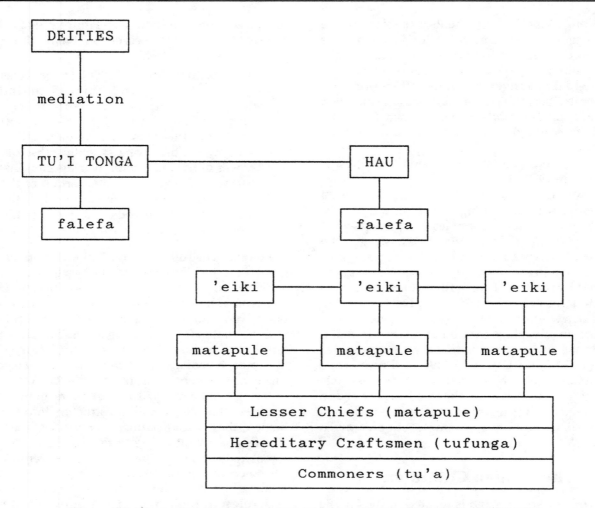

Figure 2.3. The political structure of the Tongan chiefdom (after Kirch 1983:231).

Tonga combined traditional grading of ranks by relative seniority [patrilineally] with a pattern of bilateral ranking based upon the constant superiority of a sister's to a brother's line. The first established the basis for public or general rank; the second modified deferences and respects owed to general rank within the domestic sphere.

The head of the family was the eldest male, and was succeeded by his younger brother or eldest child (Gifford 1929:20).

This patrilineal ranking between fathers and sons, older brothers and younger brothers, was reproduced in the political hierarchy of Tonga, and formed a base for legitimating power. As Gifford (1929:19) tells us

Ranking of individuals within the Tongan family...is the key to the organization of Tongan society in every stratum. From the bottom to top and from top to bottom of

the social ladder one general scheme of family organization prevails. As the Tui Tonga is *eiki* (chief) to his younger brothers, so in every Tongan family the older brother is chief to his younger brothers....Relatively speaking, in every household there are chiefs and commoners.

The reproduction of this system of generational ranking throughout the Tongan political hierarchy is obvious in the nature of political relationships:

Titled chiefs stand in certain fixed relationship to one another. Thus Ata, the "dean" of the Tongan chiefs is "grandfather" (kui) to all of the chiefs in the kingdom, except the Haa Ngata Motua chiefs, to whom he is "older brother" (taokete)....These are not true relationships, even though considered as extensions of terms for lineal relatives to collateral relatives. They are, if anything, mirrors of the relationships in which the first title bearers stood to one another (Gifford 1929:128).

Indeed, all Tongan chiefs considered themselves related to one another and all claimed descent from the Tui Tonga (Goldman 1970:290).

Taboos associated with cross-generational relationships within patrilineages were also reproduced in parallel relationships within the political hierarchy. Gifford (1929:18) explains that "It is taboo to touch a father's head or hair, to touch him while he is eating, to sleep on his bed or pillow, to partake of his food or drink, and to play with his belongings." The result of breaking one of these taboos was illness or death. Similarly, Tongan chiefs were surrounded by taboos, and the Tui Tonga was effectively removed from the rest of society by the taboos surrounding him: "when Tui Tonga entered a house it could no longer be occupied by its owner. Nobody could eat, drink, or sleep in the house in which he did" (Goldman 1970:294-95). Goldman (1970:296) tells us that

> the obligations of kinship parallel so fully those of royal tapu that regardless of the apparent logic suggesting categorical distinctions between chiefs (spiritually akin to gods) and nonchiefs, each family or household may be regarded as a minor kingdom or small congregation. As such, it offered in its own domestic domain the honors and the appearances of sanctity enjoyed by chiefs.

Primogeniture, Marriage, and Power

As in the Kongo kingdom, power in Tonga was held, at all levels, by social elders. In the family, the eldest member served as head. Lineage chiefs were considered the socially eldest in the lineage. Higher chiefs were "grandfather" or "older brother" to lesser chiefs. And all the chiefs were descended from the Tui Tonga. Also as in Kongo, the power elders had over subordinates was derived from their control of esoteric knowledge and prestige-goods.

In terms of esoteric knowledge, social elders knew more about Tongan society than their subordinates:

> Undoubtedly the chiefs and the matapule are far better informed than are the commoners. A man and wife on Nomuka Island who gave me a considerable amount of information advanced their opinions with some diffidence and apologetically said, "We do not know everything, because we are only matapule people. You should go to the chiefs" (Gifford 1929:108).

Indeed the term for commoners, tua, "is applicable to any person, even a chief or matapule, who is not 'clever in Tongan ways,' who does not act according to the prescribed Tongan etiquette, or who is rude or boorish" (Gifford 1929:108).

Social knowledge was learned from superiors, and inheritance was supposed to go to the eldest son. But this direct primogeniture could be bypassed if the person did not have the necessary qualities to carry on the father's role. In some cases, even women came to head households (Gifford 1929:20). Perhaps the most obvious example of bypassing primogeniture was in the inheritance of artisan skills and titles, known as *tufunga*. As Gifford (1929:145) tells us

> If the male members in the family of a *tufunga* lack aptitude, ambition, or any other quality, or show decided inferiority in comparison with someone outside of the family, this outsider, following a presentation of gifts to the *tufunga* (from the applicant's family), may be chosen to succeed to the order.

With the tufunga, primogeniture could be overridden. The knowledge needed by younger lineage members to succeed into higher positions in the political hierarchy was controlled by elders. They had the ability, at least in theory, to prevent the person in line of succession from gaining that knowledge.

One must keep in mind, however, that primogeniture was only crucial to ranking within the lineage. Lineage chiefs were elders, and younger members were commoners within the lineage. But within the larger political system of Tonga, status as elder or youth was not the product of simple primogeniture, but of long-term descent:

> a commoner is an individual who by virtue of descent through a series of younger brothers has in the course of generations become further and further removed from the patriarchal head of the family, as represented by a continuous line of successive eldest sons (Gifford 1929:20).

Gifford (1929:112) reiterates this point several times, stressing the importance of generational ranking in the Tonga political system:

> Because of primogeniture, it is obvious that the descendants of younger siblings sink in rank. The commoner is the man in a line of descent that gets further and further from the head of the lineage with each succeeding generation.

A Tongan's social position was relatively fixed. Although there was some room for movement, the status of his lineage, his parents, and his birth-order, all more-or-less determined his status. The potential status of his children, his grandchildren, and, in the long run his lineage, were, however, dependent upon marriages. By continuously "marrying up" in the Tongan hierarchy, an individual's children, grandchildren, and lineage could slowly increase their status. Just as a commoner was the product of a long line of younger brothers, so a chief was the product of a long line of elder siblings. The goal of Tongan marriage was to keep one's relatives marrying elders.

Prestige-Goods and Marriage Alliances

Prestige-goods were a vital part of Tongan marriage alliances, and hence, were vital to an individual's ability to marry well. Prestige-goods in Tonga were controlled at the highest level, by the Tui Tonga and the Tui Kanokupolu. They flowed down the levels of hierarchy, and were a central force in maintaining hierarchical relationships. Kirch (1984:238) makes this point very clear:

> Tonga stands unique among the indigenous Polynesian chiefdoms for its extensive and regular long-distance exchange relations with societies beyond its own geographic and political borders. This long-distance exchange had political consequences which were far greater than any immediate, utilitarian gain due to the importation of exotic material items. Long-distance exchange of chiefly spouses as well as of material items was fundamentally a political strategy, and played a vital role in binding the core islands and outliers to the central polity.

Marriage payments, and the social prestige that went along with them, were described in detail by Gifford (1929:192-93):

> Preceding the day of the beginning of the [wedding] ceremony, the fathers of the bride and groom each assembled a large gift, including tapa, mats, and oil. The particular father notified all his relatives and all his wife's relatives of the coming ceremony and asked for contributions....In distributing the presents, the bridegroom's father or other official representative of his people...had in mind what each person had donated toward the present that had been given to the bride's people, and each got

his original gift returned in double quantity. In accomplishing this return, the distributor often stripped his own house of all its material property. If he should fail to complete the traditional renumeration to all concerned, his unmarried sons and daughters and the progeny of his married children lost face and might consequently fail to contract desirable marriages....A similar distribution was made of the presents of the bridegroom's people to the bride's people.

> If there was great inequality in the size of the wedding gifts, the group making the smaller donation was shamed and lost social prestige to the other group.

In Tongan society, where marriage with an eldest son or daughter virtually determined the status of one's children, grandchildren, and lineage, there was tremendous pressure to meet marriage payments and to make them extravagant, so that one's descendants would not lose rank through a poor marriage. Since prestige-goods were needed for these payments, and the payments made possible marriage with a socially elder individual, those who controlled prestige-goods controlled individuals' abilities to socially reproduce themselves, as Kirch (1984:241) makes clear:

> Kinship alliances linked the paramount lines with those of the local ruling chiefs in the core islands and outliers. Such alliances were confirmed by marriage relations, for which exotic prestige goods were vital. In turn, the outlying islands affirmed their inferior status and loyalty to the *hau* [Tui Kanokupolu] and the Tui Tonga through the tribute of the *'inasi*. Thus within the chiefdom there was a circular flow of goods, tribute inwards towards the paramounts, prestige goods outwards to the local chiefs. Monopolization of the sources of prestige goods by the paramounts helped to secure their power over the system as a whole.

Indeed, interaction with foreign polities was also used as a means to arrange marriages that were socially acceptable. One problem in Tongan social hierarchy, that the sister of a Tui Tonga, particularly an elder sister, had a higher status than the Tui Tonga, was overcome by marrying her to a Fijian chief (Kirch 1984:238). On the other hand, high-ranking chiefs might marry, or have their sons marry, women from Samoa in order to avoid "marrying down" in the Tongan hierarchy (Kirch 1984:238; also see Kaeppler

1978). Thus, as Kirch (1984:238) points out, "underlying the more overt exchanges of goods was a system of kinship relations, with both Fiji and Samoa serving as spouse-givers to Tonga."

In short, exchanges with Fiji and Samoa, whether for prestige-goods or women, were crucial to Tongan politics. They allowed high-ranking individuals to marry well, and they brought prestige-goods into the Tongan system which allowed individuals to compete for desirable marriage arrangements. In Tonga, the chiefs did not control one's ability to survive materially, but to reproduce socially. They controlled the prestige-goods needed to make important marriage alliances that would maintain or increase the status of one's descendants. The control of prestige-goods traded from Fiji and Samoa, and in turn, the control of subordinate's ability to arrange important marriages, was the basis of political power in Tonga:

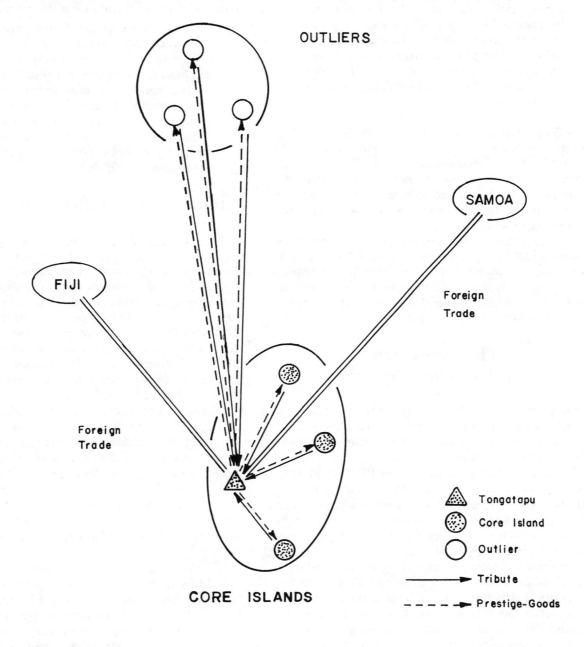

Figure 2.4. Foreign trade and political ties in Tonga (after Kirch 1983:241).

The material goods brought from Fiji and Samoa to Tonga were not by-and-large utilitarian objects, nor were they necessarily made of materials scarce in Tonga...prestige items, however, such as the red feathers, sandalwood, and fine mats were valued *koloa*, prestige items vital to Tongan marriage alliances....The acquisition of foreign prestige goods by the central polity thus served the important function of binding local chiefs to the political core. Control and redistribution of the *koloa* by the paramount lines was one strategy for binding the outer islands to the central polity (Kirch 1984:240; also see Figure 2.4).

In Tonga one perceives a situation similar to that in Kongo. Social elders controlled prestige-goods needed by their subordinates to socially reproduce themselves. A dependency relationship thereby existed between elders and subordinates, that served to keep the elders in power and able to control younger members of society.

Tonga, although on a much smaller scale than Kongo (25,000 people as opposed to 2-3 million), is still a rather complex political system. Less complex prestige-good systems are also evident in the ethnographic literature, and one of the most well described is on the Melanesian island of Karavar.

The Karavaran Prestige-Good System

Karavar is the southernmost of the Duke of York Islands, lying between New Britain and New Ireland just off the coast of Papua New Guinea. Karavar Island is about one square mile in area, and is inhabited by about 225 people (Errington 1974:14). Most of the island is planted with coconut trees, and there are some small plots of yams and greens (Errington 1974:14). The Karavarans also use portions of neighboring islands for crops, and fishing is a major source of food (Errington 1974:14).

Karavaran political structure is quite different from that of either Tonga or Kongo. In both those societies, the political structure was a mirror of the structure of localized lineages. In Karavar, however, there are no lineages. Society is organized around big men who create all-male ceremonial groups, called *apik*, recruiting membership from the men in their matrilineal moiety:

Social organization itself depends upon the personal power that Big Men exercise, for

Big Men control other people through *divara* [shell "money"], creating *apik* and social prestige in the process. The social groupings that they form rest on *them*, not on some structuring of offices that endure regardless of the personnel who fill it (Errington 1977:36).

Although matrilineal moieties exist in Karavar, the basic social and political unit is the big man's apik:

Karavar's basic political units are groupings of Big Men and their followers. The core members of these groupings are the Big Man's immediate matrilineal relatives. To this core, other men within the same moiety may add themselves, attracted by a need for protection or for *divara* ('shell money'). The groupings, called *apik*, can properly be regarded as kin groupings (Errington 1977:25-26).

Political Power and Divara

Divara consists of tiny cowrie shells strung together on strips of cane (Errington 1977:26). The standard length is a fathom, measured as a loop from the hand to the center of the chest and back to the hand (Errington 1974:22), although divara is infinitely divisible into smaller amounts (Errington 1977:26). Divara shells reputedly come from New Britain, and cannot be found on Karavar or the surrounding islands (Errington 1977:26). Karavarans acquire divara by selling crops, fish, or providing ritual services (Errington 1974:22). Anyone can acquire small amounts of divara, and indeed, all do (Errington 1977:26). However, "the purchase of a bride and the obligatory distribution of divara at a relative's funeral require quantities of divara that are often beyond the means of a young man" (Errington 1977:26-27).

Big men in Karavar are accumulators and controllers of divara. Through inheritance, careful investment, and hard work, big men acquire large amounts of divara, and through it, followers and power:

a young man will attach himself to a Big Man in his own moiety who has the supplies of divara to pay for brideprice or to distribute it at a funeral. By providing divara on these occasions, a Big Man enhances his reputation for generosity....A Big Man's power over his followers depends on whether he can and does provide divara when needed, and his cleverness in using it to control their actions (Errington 1977:27).

In order to understand big men's control over others through divara, one must first understand the Karavaran view of the world. For them, human nature is *momboto*: "greedy, formless, wild" (Errington 1977:29). Divara creates order out of momboto society by establishing social relationships, laws, and fines:

> Order is based on divara...without which there is no society but only anarchy. Sex, for instance, could not be regulated without divara: There could be no bride-price, no fines for adultery, indeed no possible definition of what was adultery, since marriage could not exist (Errington 1977:29).

For the Karavarans "divara makes society possible by channeling human nature—greed for women, for food, for prestige—into social forms: apik, marriage, adoption, and Big Man-ship" (Errington 1977:30).

Big men, by accumulating divara, cannot control society, but only influence or persuade their followers:

> A Big Man who controls his followers through divara is himself constrained through the medium, for there are not legitimate social means of controlling other people except through inducements of divara (Errington 1977:30).

Big men, however, are also able to influence their followers through their special knowledge of the *tubuan* spirit, (indeed, they are often called tubuans themselves [Errington 1974:253]). This parallels Meillassoux's theory of political power in African self-sustaining societies. Recall Meillassoux's argument that elders controlled youths through their control of prestige-goods needed for marriage and other ritual payments, and through their control of esoteric knowledge needed by young men to advance through the society's status levels. This is exactly what occurs on Karavar: big men control their followers through their control of divara and their knowledge of the tubuan—things all men who want status must acquire.

Ritual Grades on Karavar

There are five ritual grades on Karavar, three of which all men enter, another which most men enter, and a fifth which men enter in order to gain respect and prestige. Any young man who desires political power, or who aspires to become a big man, must enter all five ritual grades. Each of these ritual grades requires some outlay of divara (in increasing sums as one moves through the grades), but all basically center on the acquisition of esoteric knowledge from previously initiated men. In the final grade, this knowledge is controlled exclusively by powerful elder men, generally big men. It is through their control of this esoteric knowledge that elders solidify their control over youths, and big men solidify their control over their followers.

The first ritual grade is entered when a young man is taken to the men's ground, or *taraiu*, for the first time (Errington 1974:79). The taraiu is located on a 400 yard stretch of beach and extends about 100 yards into the forest (Errington 1974:79). The boy is ceremonially taken away from his mother and the other village women, who defend him from the men with sticks, and spends several weeks at the taraiu (Errington 1974:79). During this time he eats only food prepared by men at the taraiu, and is kept completely secluded from any contact with women (Errington 1974:85).

The next ritual grade is entered when a young man is shown that a tubuan figure is not really a spirit, but a man dressed as one (although a tubuan is still extremely powerful [Errington 1974:80]). In a similar vein, the young man enters the third ritual grade when he is shown that the other Karavaran spirit figure, the *dukduk*, is also a dressed-up man (Errington 1974:80). Frederick Errington (1974:89) gives this description of the revealing of a tubuan:

> The tubuan was kneeling, surrounded by men seated in a circle. They boys entered this circle, dropped their lengths of divara in front of the kneeling tubuan and sat and nervously ate a few bites of their food. After a few minutes, the tubuan jumped to its feet and the boys fled, only to be caught by the men who still surrounded them. The tubuan danced for a bit, then suddenly removed its uppermost portion, revealing the face of the carrier, a fellow Karavaran. Then the tubuan removed its entire costume, layer by layer, so that the boys could see its construction and the way it was worn.

Errington (1974:80) also explains that

> Once a boy has gone to the taraiu, it is inevitable that he "see" the tubuan and the dukduk [since they are manufactured there and he will be expected to help in their manufacture]. These three steps are linked, are inexpensive, and are necessary for minimal ritual participation.

Dukduks and tubuans are basically large, hollow cone-shaped masks (see Figure 2.5). The physical masks are not purchased, only the copyright to a particular design (Errington 1974:80). The masks themselves are only made when needed for *mata-matam* rituals (discussed below), and the magic

PNP

Figure 2.5. A Tubuan (after Errington 1974).

necessary to create a mask is also part of the purchase. Indeed, for the tubuan, the purchase of magic necessary to control it is perhaps the most important part (as I will discuss below). Errington (1974:181) offers this description of how these ritual costumes are constructed:

> The stems of the leaves were fastened together into hoops so that the leaves all hung in one direction. Fastened to the bottom hoop was a pair of vine strap

suspenders. To don a dukduk or tubuan, a man squirms into the bottom hoop, fits the suspenders over his shoulders, and then piles on layers of additional leaf hoops until they reach eye level. On top of all this he holds the head of the dukduk or tubuan securely on his shoulders by means of his uplifted but concealed hands.

The fourth ritual grade is entered when a young man purchases a dukduk. This requires much more divara than any of the other three grades: entering the first three grades may have cost about 30 fathoms of divara, but buying a dukduk costs between 60 and 100 fathoms (Errington 1974:93). Although a young man should, in theory, be able to recover all the divara he puts into the purchase of a dukduk (Errington 1974:91), an initial outlay is still necessary. If a young man's father cannot or will not put up the divara necessary for the purchase of a dukduk, a young man will have to seek out a sponsor, often a big man (see Errington 1974:91-97).

Despite the expense, virtually every male purchases a dukduk (Errington 1974:91). The reason is twofold: first, a man who has not bought a dukduk is not considered to be fully male; and second, a man is not supposed to marry until he buys one (Errington 1974:100).

Very few men, however, purchase a tubuan. To do so is to ritually differentiate oneself from other men, and to make the first step towards becoming a big man (Errington 1974:91). To do so also requires a considerable outlay of divara, not only for the purchase of the tubuan pattern, but, more importantly, to be taught the magic necessary to control the tubuan. The choice of a teacher is vital:

> A man who buys the tubuan is able, assuming other necessary characteristics, to become a big man and thus to become a possible rival to the established big man. It would be a mistake, therefore, to ask an adept to take a class if he felt his position was threatened. He might, by refusing to accept the class, humiliate those who had approached him; he might even attack with sorcery these men who were thus showing themselves as potential rivals; or, worst of all, he might accept the class but intentionally teach incorrect or incomplete spells which would not protect a man against the power of the tubuan...As a consequence, they desire to find a teacher who is trustworthy and has a reputation for knowing high quality spells (Errington 1974:111-112).

Therefore, most young men align themselves with well-established big men when they want to purchase a tubuan. In doing so they reinforce the big man's status and position while advancing their own. This, again, gets back to Meillassoux: social elders (big men in this case) not only subordinate social youths through the control of prestige goods (divara) and esoteric knowledge (tubuan magic), but use that subordination to display and maintain their own status.

Matamatam, Tubuan, and Big Men

The ability to control a tubuan is the defining characteristic of a Karavaran big man (Errington 1974:118). The display of this control over tubuan, as well as the display of supplies of divara necessary to be considered a big man, take place at the mortuary ceremony of matamatam (Errington 1974:98). As Errington (1974:99) tells us, "An individual will sponsor a matamatam so that he will be recognized or confirmed as a big man".

A matamatam is used to "finish" a moiety's dead. When the dead are "finished," the living no longer have to think about them (Errington 1974:122). This has an important significance for an aspiring big man, for if he wants to take the place of a dead big man, he must formally allow the dead big man's followers to "forget" him, and ally themselves with the living big man (Errington 1974:122). As Errington (1974:22) explains:

> A big man gives existence to an apik; consequently his followers are adrift after his death. Only when these followers are incorporated into an apik focused on another big man can their former big man be forgotten; only then is he finished. Finishing the dead involves the replacement of one big man by another big man.

The ability to replace or "finish" a big man requires an individual to demonstrate his control of two things: divara and tubuan (in more general terms, prestige-goods and esoteric knowledge). As Errington tells us, "The matamatam is a proving ground for a big man; at this time he demonstrates that he does control followers and that he does control the tubuan" (1974:123). He later explains that "the matamatam provides a series of tests and, in some cases, ordeals, that require a sponsor to prove publicly he is a big man" (1974:224). The control of followers is evidenced through an aspiring big man's ability to get the matamatam organized (Errington 1974:225). His control of the tubuan is evidenced through three major acts: painting the tubuan's eyes; striking the tubuan with divara; and sending off the tubuan spirit.

When the tubuan's eyes are painted "it becomes animated: it can see and can, if treated imprudently, kill. When the adept paints the eyes he is bringing back the tubuan's wild and dangerous spirit...and bringing it under human control" (Errington 1974:166-67). When the aspiring big man strikes the tubuan with divara

> If he does not utter the proper spell the tubuan will kill him. If the sponsor survives this encounter, it demonstrates very explicitly that he is indeed a big man: he is one who controls the tubuan/society with divara (Errington 1974:224-25).

Finally, when the aspiring big man releases the tubuan spirit, he is only in danger if the spirit feels the tubuan was not made for sufficient reason. If the matamatam was not extravagant enough, if the sponsor did not adequately demonstrate that he controls followers and divara, the tubuan spirit will linger and kill him (Errington 1974:225). In short,

> A defining feature of a big man is his ritual capacity to bring the tubuan under control: a big man is able to domesticate its wild spirit just as he is able to constrain his followers through the use of divara. The major purpose of a matamatam is to bring the tubuan and the big man into conjunction, providing a test of a big man's power to impose order on others as shown through his control of the tubuan (Errington 1974:118).

Karavar Compared to Tonga and Kongo

The Karavaran prestige-good system is very different from the Tongan and Kongan examples, but it is in many ways the closest of all three to Meillassoux's original theory upon which the concept of a prestige-good system is based. In Karavar power is based on divara and knowledge of the ritual grades. As one proceeds through the ritual grades, moving towards the status of a social elder, one must expend divara. At the highest levels the amounts of divara necessary require a young man's alliance with an elder, reinforcing their status. As one moves through the ritual grades one also gains esoteric knowledge about the taraiu, the dukduk and tubuan, and in the highest levels, about magic with which to control the dukduk and tubuan spirits. In order to gain this knowledge, one must be taught by one's social elder, again reinforcing their status. In Karavar, a young man becomes a social elder, and gains political power, by subordinating himself to social elders, admitting and supplicating himself to their power.

In Karavar, as well, social elders control young men's access to women. According to the Karavaran norm, one must buy a dukduk before one can be married. The purchase of a dukduk requires both a large amount of divara and the acquisition of esoteric knowledge on how the dukduk is built. In order to get the divara and knowledge he requires to purchase a dukduk, a young man must ally himself and subordinate himself to a social elder, again reinforcing their status and power.

The Karavaran prestige-good system is in many ways the most obvious and "classic" example of a prestige-good system that I have been able to locate. Big men openly control others through foreign prestige-goods (divara) and esoteric knowledge (of the tubuan). As Shelly Errington (1977:37) tells us:

> while there is a sense in which Big Man's exercise of power is personal, there is another sense in which it is profoundly impersonal, for it is based not on charisma or personal appeal or magnetism, but on their stores of divara and their abilities to manipulate the divara to acquire followers. It could be argued that Karavarans do not feel any "personal" loyalty to Big Men: If a Big Man failed to provide divara when the occasion demanded, no one would remain his follower.

Errington (1977:37) is even more blatant about the power that divara carries for the Karavarans: "Power (which I will take to mean loosely "control over other people") is accomplished through a substance, divara....Power has one source....In fact, it is not that divara is a source of power so much that it is itself power."

In Karavar, prestige-goods are the embodiment of power. Those who control the prestige-goods control others through the power of the prestige-goods themselves. Although esoteric knowledge is a source of power for Karavaran big men, without the stores of divara necessary to gain that knowledge and to put on a matamatam to display it, the big man would have no power, and he would not be considered a big man. Big men's power in Karavar flows directly from their control of prestige-goods.

Common Elements in Prestige-Good Systems

By comparing these three prestige-good systems, one should be able to find elements in common; elements that may imply structures basic to all prestige-good systems. Jonathan Friedman (1982:184) has suggested that prestige-good systems share the following elements in common:

> (a) generalized exchange; (b) monopoly over prestige-good imports that are necessary for marriage and other crucial payments, i.e., for the social reproduction of local kin groups; (c) bilineal tendency in the kinship structure (asymmetrical); and (d) tendency to asymmetrical political dualism: religious-political chiefs, original people-new-comers, etc.

Certainly the first two elements are present in all prestige-good systems—they are defining elements. The other two may be present in some systems, but not in all; and Friedman leaves out some elements, most importantly the reproduction of the smallest social unit in the political structure and the emphasis on elder/younger relations, which appear to be central features of the three prestige-good systems I have considered.

In all three prestige-good systems I have looked at, generalized exchange of prestige-goods occurs. In both Kongo and Tonga foreign trade and the goods that come from it were controlled at the highest level of the political hierarchy. These were distributed down the hierarchy in return for service and tribute, but the distribution was certainly general and not reciprocal. In Karavar, although all did control some divara, big men controlled amounts beyond the potential of most individuals. This divara was given out for specific work done, to subordinates in order for them to enter ritual grades, and at rituals such as matamatam. Distribution of divara by big men was certainly generalized—in most cases all the big men got in return was prestige and the knowledge that they had strengthened their political position.

Monopoly over goods needed for marriage, initiation, and other crucial payments at the highest level of the political hierarchy is also present in all three systems. In Kongo, shell beads, raffia cloth, and other imported preciosities were needed for bridewealth payments, and these could only be obtained from the king (although they flowed down the political hierarchy so that most individuals probably got them from local chiefs or lineage heads). In Tonga "men get all their red feathers for making their ornaments & all their fine painted cloth, & figured mats & curious beaded baskets & other curious ornaments' from Fiji" (Kirch 1984:239). These goods were necessary for Tongans to make extravagant marriage payments in order to arrange status-maintaining or enhancing marriages, and they were only obtainable from the Tui's (although, as in Kongo, these goods flowed down the hierarchy, and were probably obtained by most people through local chiefs). Finally, in Karavar, divara was needed to enter the ritual grades necessary for a youth to become a man, and to be eligible for marriage. Again, although anyone could acquire divara, the amounts necessary to enter the final ritual grades could only be obtained from a sponsor, often a big man.

A bilineal tendency in kinship is also present, to some extent, in all three prestige-good systems I have considered. In Kongo, matrilineal lineages were contrasted with the patrilineal nature of the political structure. In Tonga, the matrilineal line carried status, while the patrilineal line carried political power. In Karavar, society was organized into matrilineal moieties, while the basic political units were men's groups organized around a big man. It is clear that in all three prestige-good systems there is some tendency for bilineal relationships to occur, but those relationships are highly varied between the three. There seems to be no clear-cut bilineal kinship system at work in these three prestige-good systems, and therefore bilineality may not be as important an element of prestige-good systems as Friedman states.

Rather than focusing on bilineal kinship in prestige-good systems, I believe it is more important to consider the reproduction of a society's basic kinship structure in its political hierarchy. Indeed, it may be this tendency to reproduce kinship structure in the political structure that gives rise to the apparent bilineality that Friedman perceives. The reproduction of kinship relations in the political structure is obvious and striking in all three prestige-good systems I discussed. In Kongo, the basic relationship between elder males and younger males within localized matrilineages was reproduced as a hierarchy of chiefs. Each chief was subordinate to an "elder" chief (except, of course, the king), and superordinate to a "younger" chief. These subordinate/superordinate relationships were designated by kinship terms, such as father/son and grandfather/grandson. In Tonga, a similar situation obtained, with even the taboos placed upon relationships within the lineage being reproduced in relationships within the political hierarchy. In Karavar, one can compare big men with fathers: sponsoring younger males as fathers are supposed to if they can; teaching younger males dukduk and tubuan magic, again as fathers are supposed to do if they can. Indeed, sponsorship often leads to the ritual adoption of a young man (see Errington 1974:92-98). Karavaran big men, in a sense, are a recreation of the father/son relationship in a political form.

This father/son, elder male/younger male emphasis in prestige-good systems is another important element that is overlooked by Friedman. In all three prestige-good systems I have considered, polit-

ical power is associated directly with social elders, and the means to political power lie in one's becoming a social elder. Youths are excluded from political power and prestige, and are exploited by elders to enhance their own power and prestige. To reiterate what I said above, in both Kongo and Tonga, political superiors are considered to be the social elders of their political subordinates. These relationships take on the kinship terms for elder/younger such as father/son and grandfather/grandson. In Karavar, although there is no political hierarchy, there is a hierarchy of ritual grades. Those who have entered more of the grades are social elders to those who have not, and only the eldest socially (those who have bought a tubuan) are eligible to be big men. In all three prestige-good systems, political power is directly linked to, and legitimated by, being eldest socially.

Finally, Friedman's statement that prestige-good systems tend to have asymmetrical political dualism is not well supported in the three prestige-good systems I have considered. Certainly Tonga had asymmetric political dualism between the Tui Tonga, the spiritual/religious head, and the Tui Kanokupolu, the social head, but neither Kongo nor Karavar exhibit this dualism. Indeed, both have leaders who act as combined religious/political heads. The Kongan king was the closest to the ancestors of all Kongans, yet he was also the political leader. A defining feature of the Karavaran big man was control of the tubuan spirit. Asymmetrical political dualism only occurs in one of the three prestige-good systems I have considered, and may not be an important element of prestige-good systems in general.

Conclusions

Four major elements seem to be present in all three of the prestige-good systems I discussed: (1) generalized exchange of prestige-goods; (2) monopoly over prestige-goods at the highest political level; (3) the reproduction of basic kinship structures in the political structure; and (4) political power held by the socially eldest members of society.

Political power in all three prestige-good systems is based upon the control of prestige-goods needed by members of the societies in order to pay social debts—bridewealth, initiation, fines, and the like. Because they controlled these goods, political leaders in these prestige-good systems were able to control individual's abilities to pay social debts, and hence, to socially reproduce themselves. This is the most fundamental aspect of all prestige-good systems, that those with power control other's ability to socially reproduce by controlling the means of social reproduction: prestige-goods.

Even with these major elements in common, the three prestige-good systems I considered were strikingly different in most aspects. They existed on different scales, on different levels of complexity, and on different levels of integration. The question I must ask, then, is how these systems came to be as they are.

What are the primary variables in prestige-good systems that cause change in societal scale, complexity, and integration? This is the topic of the next chapter, a consideration of social evolution in prestige-good systems.

3

Social Evolution in Prestige-Good Systems

In the last chapter I considered the structures of prestige-good systems. In this chapter I attempt to understand how those structures change, and develop a general theory of social evolution in prestige-good systems. I define social evolution following Blanton and his colleagues (1981:17) as "change in societal scale, integration, and complexity." Scale relates to size, both the number of people and the size of the geographic area considered to be part of a society (Blanton et al. 1981:17). Integration relates to the interdependence of units within a society. As Blanton and his colleagues (1981:20) explain "Higher levels of integration imply more connections among units...the connections are established as flows of material, energy, information, or people." Complexity relates to the functional differentiation among societal units, or the number of functionally distinct segments of a society (Blanton et al. 1981:21).

Existing Theories of Evolution in Prestige-Good Systems

In his book *From Stone to Steel* (1962), Richard Salisbury considers the effect introducing steel tools and other European goods had on the Siane people of highland New Guinea. The Siane clearly were part of a prestige-good system, for Salisbury (1962:190-191) tells us that

> Valuables are used to obtain free-floating power within a group, when contributed to the payment of others. The contributor gains power in the form of an increment to his informal social ranking....Another use of valuables to obtain free-floating

> power...occurs at some rites of passage.... Where the child had only a certain number of rights as the incumbent of his former position, by the giving away of valuables in his name he acquires new rights, and a new social status....Clearly, then, individuals use valuables to obtain new power or new rights....Valuables are exchanged for power.

Salisbury (1962:208) offers a theory of social evolution among the Siane stemming from the introduction of European goods. He claims that the Siane existed in a state of sociopolitical stability prior to European contact, and had been in equilibrium for at least 100 years. Within this equilibrium

> The circulation of valuables ensured that able men could gain sufficient prestige within the democratic society to carry out those tasks requiring an exercise of authority and that an approximate political balance was kept between groups. The use of luxury goods prevented undue rigidity. Capital was renewed as needed by the allocation of 2 per cent of each man's time to producing capital goods [Salisbury gives support for this figure earlier in the work], thereby maintaining both the standard of life and the indigenous structure of society (Salisbury 1962:208).

With the introduction of European tools, capital investment shrunk, and individuals used the time and energy they saved to increase their political power "either by fighting or by the use of material tokens of prestige" (Salisbury 1962:209). The end result was inflation in the "cost of power," an increasing size of individual groups, and an increase in the power of important men (Salisbury 1962:209). According to Salisbury (1962:209), if no further change occurred, this situation would result in a wealthy society "possessing a system of social statuses with little productive function but much associated ritual," similar, perhaps, to Tonga. However, this situation could also result in a larger, more centralized society, able to coordinate productive tasks and to produce more and different goods (Salisbury 1962:209), similar, perhaps, to Kongo.

Salisbury's theory has some interesting elements. Most importantly, it focuses on change stemming from the introduction of new goods. In a prestige-good system, where goods are the basis of political power, it makes sense that the introduction of new goods would alter the power structure. However, Salisbury seems to be more concerned with the time-saving elements of European-introduced goods, rather than their potential use as prestige-goods for acquiring "free-floating" power.

Jonathan Friedman has also developed a theory of social evolution in prestige-good systems based on the introduction of new goods. His theory is more focused on the potential power inherent in the new goods themselves, rather than their potential to be time-savers. Friedman is basically concerned with changes in trade density. He tells us that within a prestige-good system "The decline in political central-ization is the general threshold effect of an increase in trade density" (Friedman 1982:193). In contrast, a decrease in trade density should have the opposite effect—an increase in political centralization (Friedman 1982:192). Friedman (1982:191) also states that where agricultural intensification fails, political centralization must decline. This is similar to Renfrew's (1982:265) suggestion, discussed in Chapter 1, that intensification must accompany any increase in political centralization. Friedman's theory is modeled in Figure 3.1.

Moving from the bottom to the top of Figure 3.1, we get a picture of change through time in the polit-ical complexity of prestige-good systems given change in trade density. On the left, trade density increases, while on the right it decreases. When trade density increases, individuals within the prestige-good system have more access to prestige-goods. This leads to a breakdown of any political hierarchy based upon the monopoly of these goods, the growth of prestige competition, and finally a big-man type of political leadership. If external trade is maintained, this results in a system like that of Karavar, with pres-tige-goods and food moving in different spheres. If external trade is cut off, some types of food may them-

selves become prestige-goods, as pigs are in highland New Guinea (see Strathern 1971).

On the right side of Figure 3.1, when trade density decreases, there is a decrease in access to prestige-goods. Those who once monopolized prestige-goods compete for the goods that remain, and a chieftain-ship develops around those who are able to maintain their monopoly. If the society is able to increase subsistence production for the support of a chiefly elite, this trajectory may end up in the formation of a quasi-state, like Kongo. If, however, intensification of subsistence production is difficult or impossible, the growth of a strongly centralized power will be stifled, perhaps as on Tonga.

Trade Density and Political Complexity

Using Salisbury's and Friedman's theories as a base, it appears that four elements are central to the processes of social evolution in prestige-good systems: (1) societal scale; (2) societal boundedness; (3) volume of trade; and (4) potential for intensifica-tion. There may be some confusion here. At the beginning of this chapter I defined social evolution as change in societal scale, integration, and complexity. Here I am saying that scale is a central element in the social evolution of prestige-good systems. The confu-sion lies is taking my definition of social evolution as a theory of process, and thereby seeing societal scale as a dependent variable in social evolution. Although social evolution appears to be often accompanied by change in societal scale, societal scale need not be a variable in theories of social evolution, and should not be considered as one in the definition of social evolu-tion given earlier in this chapter. In the theory of social evolution I develop below, however, societal scale is an important variable.

Of the four variables that appear central to social evolution in prestige-good systems, the potential for intensification is perhaps the least active. It is simply a limiting factor on the development of political complexity. Again recalling Renfrew, no movement towards political complexity can be made without intensification. Political intensification and economic intensification must go hand in hand; there can be no elites without intensification of production to support them.

The other three elements central to the processes of social evolution in prestige-good systems relate to what Friedman calls "trade density." If one defines trade density as a measure of the number of prestige-goods per capita in a population during a given period of time, then a change in any of these three elements will directly effect trade density. One can state this relationship as an equation:

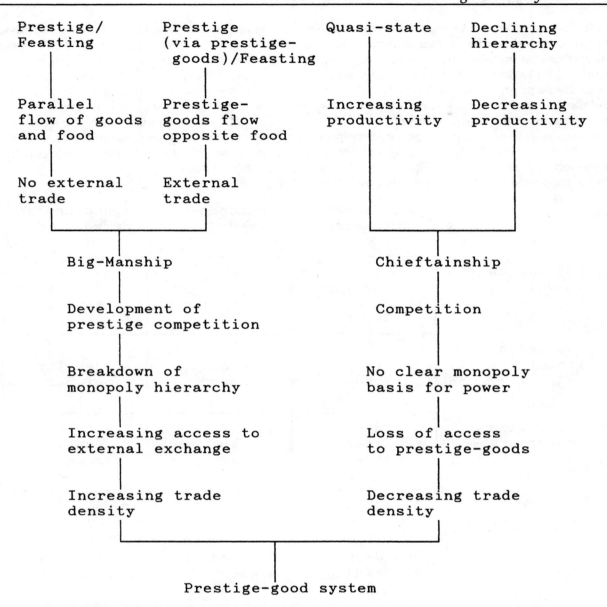

Figure 3.1. Friedman's theory of social evolution in prestige-good systems (adapted from Friedman 1982:192).

Equation 3.1: $\Sigma\,G/P{*}U = \Sigma\,G/T + \Sigma\,T/U * 1/P$

Where

G = Prestige-goods entering the system.

P = The population of the system.

U = The unit of time during which the measurement of trade density is being made.

T = Transactions made to obtain prestige-goods.

In Equation 3.1, $\Sigma\,G/T$ represents the volume of trade in prestige-goods (the number of prestige-goods obtained per transaction); $\Sigma\,T/U$ represents the system's boundedness (the number of transactions per unit time); and $1/P$ is the inverse of the population. One can turn this equation into a measure of instantaneous trade density by dropping out the time element. The equation then becomes:

Equation 3.2: $\Sigma\,G/P = \Sigma\,G/T * \Sigma\,T/P$

Equations 3.1 and 3.2 explain a good deal about the nature of trade density in prestige-good systems.

Trade density is directly proportional to the number of prestige-goods in the system and the number of transactions taking place to obtain prestige-goods. However, trade density is inversely proportional to the system's population—if the population grows (and the other factors remain constant), the density of prestige-goods in the system will drop.

If social evolution in prestige-good systems is brought about by changes in trade density, as suggested by Friedman, then Equations 3.1 and 3.2 offer a good model of the changes that might occur given fluctuation in scale, boundedness, and the volume of trade in prestige-goods. The relationships between these variables and trade density are summarized in Figures 3.2, 3.3, and 3.4. By combining volume of trade with boundedness one can create a new variable that relates to "trade flow" (simply $\Sigma\,G/U$, or the number of prestige-goods entering a system in any given unit of time). The relationship between scale, trade flow, and trade density is shown in Figure 3.5.

	Boundedness increasing	Boundedness steady	Boundedness decreasing
Population increasing	density much lower	density lower	density steady
Population steady	density lower	density steady	density higher
Population decreasing	density steady	density higher	density much higher

Figure 3.2. The relationship between scale, boundedness, and trade density.

	Boundedness increasing	Boundedness steady	Boundedness decreasing
Volume of trade increasing	density steady	density higher	density much higher
Volume of trade steady	density lower	density steady	density higher
Volume of trade decreasing	density much lower	density lower	density steady

Figure 3.3. The relationship between volume of trade, boundedness, and trade density.

According to Friedman's theory, a decrease in trade density brings about increasing political complexity in prestige-good systems (Figure 3.1). This makes sense given the nature of prestige-good systems. Power in prestige-good systems is based upon the control of imported prestige-goods. If the density of these goods decreases, those who have them and control them should gain power, as their power is based on the scarcity of the goods they control. As long as prestige-goods remain necessary for social reproduction, the power of those controlling them will grow as their density declines. Of course, the growth of their power and of political complexity is limited by the society's ability to intensify production to support them.

An increase in trade density, according to Friedman's theory, should result in a decrease in the political complexity of the prestige-good system. This too makes sense given the nature of prestige-good systems. If a system is flooded with prestige-goods,

	Volume of trade increasing	Volume of trade steady	Volume of trade decreasing
Population increasing	density steady	density lower	density much lower
Population steady	density higher	density steady	density lower
Population decreasing	density much higher	density higher	density steady

Figure 3.4. The relationship between scale, volume of trade, and trade density.

	Trade flow increasing	Trade flow steady	Trade flow decreasing
Population increasing	density steady	density lower	density much lower
Population steady	density higher	density steady	density lower
Population decreasing	density much higher	density higher	density steady

Figure 3.5. The relationship between scale, trade flow, and trade density.

the control of them is meaningless. Alliances with individuals who control prestige-goods are not necessary if individuals have easy access to them. Therefore, as trade density increases, the power of those controlling prestige-goods decreases.

In a similar vein, when the density of prestige-goods increases, it gives opportunities for accumulating prestige-goods to more people, again undermining the power base of those controlling them. This is exactly what occurred in Kongo with the coming of Europeans. On the other hand, when the density of prestige-goods decreases, it gives the most powerful in the system the opportunity to consolidate their power, driving competitors who are not able to maintain access to prestige-goods out of the power structure.

The power of those individuals who control prestige-goods in a system is therefore directly related to the density of the goods in the system. From this relationship one can devise a figure similar to Figure 3.5 that relates societal scale and trade flow with the power of political leaders in prestige-good systems, as shown in Figure 3.6. From Figure 3.6 one can see that if population decreases and trade flow increases, the power of those controlling prestige-goods in the system will decrease. Similarly, if population increases and trade flow decreases, the power of those controlling prestige-goods will increase. The increase of political centralization or hierarchy will, again, be limited by the society's ability to intensify production for the support of these prestige-good controllers.

Figure 3.6 is a model of one theory of prestige-good system process. The remainder of this chapter consists of an evaluation of this theory and of the relationship between political centralization and trade density in prestige-good systems. By considering several prestige-good systems in the process of change, one should be able to determine whether the elements I have been discussing (scale, boundedness, and volume of trade) are indeed active in the processes of social evolution within prestige-good systems. The societies I examine are the Kwakiutl, the Kiriwina Islanders, and European Catholics in the Middle Ages. Their approximate positions in the structure of Figure 3.6 is given as Figure 3.7.

The Kwakiutl Prestige-Good System

When first contacted by Europeans, the Kwakiutl inhabited the northern part of Vancouver Island and the adjacent mainland of southwestern British Columbia. The climate of this region is mild and wet, and there is an abundance of land and sea animals and forest products. Because the coastal mountains come right down to the sea and are covered with thick cedar forests, the Kwakiutl lived directly on the coast and were ocean-oriented peoples (see Codere 1950:1).

Kwakiutl society was organized around a bilineal lineage form called a *numaym*. Stuart Piddocke (1969:136) explains that the numaym:

	Trade flow increasing	Trade flow steady	Trade flow decreasing
Population increasing	power steady	power greater	power much greater
Population steady	power lesser	power steady	power greater
Population decreasing	power much less	power lesser	power steady

Figure 3.6. The relationship between scale, trade flow, and the power of political leaders in prestige-good systems.

may be summarily described as a named group associated mythologically with a traditional place of origin; it owned property consisting of fishing locations, hunting territory, and one or more houses in winter villages; and it was headed by a chief or headman descended, at least in theory, in the most senior genealogical line from a founding ancestor. The members of the numaym consisted of people related, sometimes closely, sometimes distantly, usually patrilineally, but often through their mothers or wives, to the chief.

Within each numaym there were a number of ranked positions or "seats" (Boas 1966:50). Indeed, Franz Boas (1966:50) tells us that

> The structure of the numayma [*sic*] is best understood if we disregard the living individuals and rather consider the numayma as consisting of a certain number of positions...[these] are the skeleton of the numayma, and individuals, in the course of their lives, may occupy various positions.

The means of maintaining or increasing one's position in the numaym was through a competitive ceremony of wealth distribution and destruction known as the potlatch. Power was based on success in potlatching. Helen Codere (1950:63) described the potlatch in this way:

The Kwakiutl potlatch is the ostentatious and dramatic distribution of property by the holder of a fixed, ranked, and named position to other position holders. The purpose is to validate the hereditary claim to the position and to live up to it by maintaining its relative glory and rank against the rivalrous claims of the others.

Piddocke (1969:146) adds that

> the more generous the host was, the more prestige he received; and if his generosity was not matched by the guests when they gave their potlatches, the host and his numaym increased in prestige at the expense of the guests.

Potlatches were given for an individual's birth, naming, acquisition of a numaym position, initiation into secret societies, marriage, death, or simply because the individual had accumulated a lot of property and wanted to gain prestige for himself and his numaym (Codere 1950:63; Piddocke 1969:146-47).

Since power was obtained through the giving of potlatches, numaym chiefs were the main potlatch givers. Indeed, Piddocke (1969:131,137) argues that in the past, potlatching was the primary function of numaym chiefs. However, from all historic accounts, potlatching was done by everyone, and was the basis of Kwakiutl social structure (Curtis 1915:141). The Kwakiutl had an extreme desire to gain social prestige: "Scarcely a phase of their activities can be

	Trade flow increasing	Trade flow steady	Trade flow decreasing
Population increasing		Medieval Catholics	
Population steady			Kiriwina Islanders
Population decreasing	Kwakiutl		

Figure 3.7. The location of societies to be considered in Chapter 3 in relation to scale and trade flow.

discussed without reference to this idea, and in fact their entire existence is an endless scheming and striving to enhance their individual standing" (Curtis 1915:137). And the means to gain prestige was through the potlatch: "the method of acquiring rank...is done by means of the potlatch" (Boas 1966:77).

The Kwakiutl are therefore an excellent example of an aboriginal North American prestige-good system. Power was related to success in the potlatch, and the potlatch was basically a display and distribution of prestige-goods. Before European contact, these goods consisted of various skin blankets and cedar-bark blankets, but after contact woolen blankets became the standard for exchange. Both before and after contact, beaten sheets of copper in a standard form and decorated with animal motifs were imported from societies to the north. These "coppers" were the most valuable and prestigious goods given away or destroyed at potlatches.

The Kwakiutl also manifest other characteristics common to the prestige-good systems I described in the last chapter. There is generalized exchange of prestige-goods (indeed, there is a system of compounded interest inherent in potlatch exchanges—see Codere 1950). Prestige-goods are monopolized at the highest level of the political hierarchy, by numaym position-holders and chiefs. The basic structure of the numaym, a system of ranked positions held together through loosely-defined kinship bonds, is reproduced in the relationships of individual numayms to each other in villages, and between villages in the Kwakiutl region as a whole. As Piddocke (1969:141) tells us "The numayms within a tribe were also ranked in serial order, the head of the highest ranking numaym being reckoned the head chief of the tribe or village," and Codere (1950:2) "Each tribe was ranked in greatness in relation to all other tribes." Finally, political power was held by the socially eldest members of society, numaym chiefs.

Change in the Kwakiutl Potlatch

With the coming of Europeans, not only did the major goods exchanged in potlatches shift, but the amount of goods exchanged increased dramatically as well. Figure 3.8 shows the increase in the number of blankets (both woolen and fur or cedar) exchanged in potlatches from roughly 1729 to 1936. It is clear that there was an almost exponential increase in the number of blankets given away after about 1850, and this dramatic increase correlates well with the introduction of woolen blankets into the potlatch (Codere 1950:94-96). The overall material wealth of the Kwakiutl also increased during this time, mainly

through wage-labor and the sale of fish and other goods to Canadians. Codere (1950:43) tells us that "The increase in the money income of the Kwakiutl during the first two decades of the twentieth century was a major factor in the historical development of Kwakiutl culture. Per capita earnings increased from $54 in 1903 to $244 in 1921." Her graphs showing the increasing value of Kwakiutl private dwellings and personal property are reproduced as Figure 3.9.

At the same time that the volume of goods moving through the Kwakiutl culture was increasing, the numbers of the Kwakiutl themselves were declining rapidly. Smallpox, measles, and other diseases helped to drive a rapid and continuous decline in Kwakiutl population (Codere 1950:49-61). The decline in Kwakiutl population from contact to 1934 is presented in Figure 3.10.

It should be obvious that this situation, declining population and increasing flow of goods, fits well into the theory of prestige-good system process presented in Figure 3.6. This situation should result in a dramatic increase in trade density, and an equally dramatic decline in the power of political leaders accompanied by fierce competition for political power.

Competition for political power within the Kwakiutl prestige-good system during this time is clear. In fact the increase in the amount of goods being given away at potlatches is a clear indication of this competition. At the highest levels, this competition lead to extreme displays of wealth. Tables 3.1 and 3.2 show this competition plainly through the increase in both the size of the largest potlatches held from 1849 to 1949, and in the number of large potlatches held.

Piddocke argues that prior to European contact the potlatch was much different than that described by Boas and Codere. Two of his claims for change from the pre-contact to the post-contact potlatch also support the idea of growing competition for prestige. First, Piddocke (1969:131) claims that the pre-contact potlatch involved chiefs only, and hence was an inter-numaym or inter-tribal competition. Prestige was gained only for the numaym or tribe, not for the individual. This changed following European contact, and the potlatch became one of inter-personal rivalry (Codere 1950:63-66). Secondly, Piddocke (1969:145-46) claims that the destruction of property so prevalent in Boas's and Codere's descriptions of the potlatch was also a modern development. The extreme action of destroying one's wealth (gaining immense prestige in the process), stemmed from newly heightened competition following European contact and the need for high-ranking individuals to create new and awesome displays of wealth and power. In Piddocke's (1969:152) view the destruction of property also

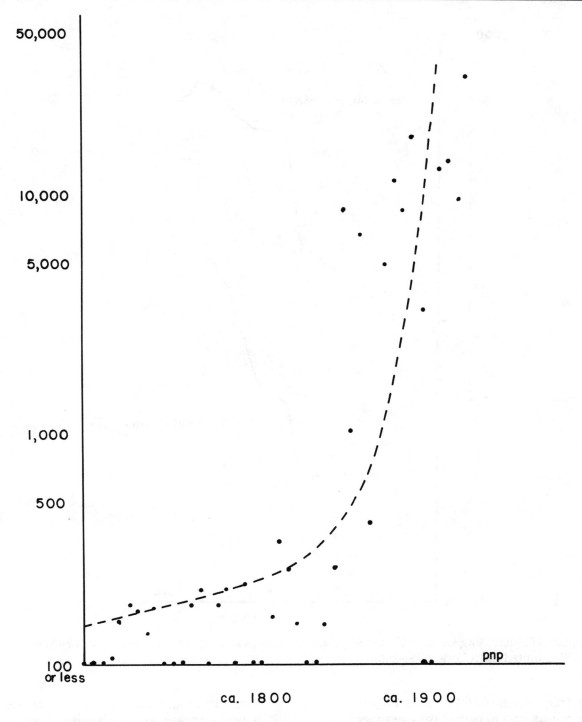

Figure 3.8. Blankets distributed at forty-four Kwakiutl potlatches between 1729 and 1936 (adapted from Codere 1950:90-91).

served to take wealth out of the system and hence decrease trade density.

Interestingly, Piddocke's conclusions about modern change in the Kwakiutl potlatch parallel those suggested by the theory of social evolution in prestige-good I systems developed earlier in this chapter. As he (Piddocke 1969:152) tells us

The entry into the system of a new, non-traditional source of wealth: The general effect of this factor would be to promote

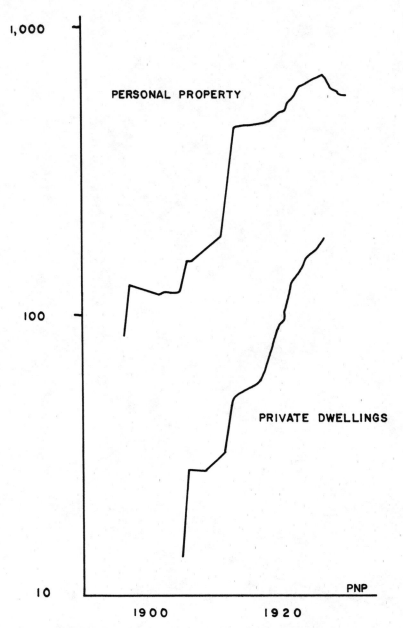

Figure 3.9. Increasing value of Kwakiutl private dwellings and personal property from 1900 to 1930 (adapted from Codere 1950:48).

more frequent potlatches and bigger potlatch gifts, and to permit persons other than the traditional chiefs to engage in potlatching. This in turn would promote an increase in competitive or rivalrous potlatching. Exchanges would become less between numayms and more between prestige-seeking individuals....A general decline in population...would both free more wealth...for use in potlatching and increase the per capita wealth among the

Kwakiutl. Frequency and size of potlatches would increase, and with this increased wealth the chances of more persons being engaged in it would also be increased.

The Kwakiutl, then, appear to support the theory of prestige-good system evolution I developed earlier in this chapter. As trade flow increased and Kwakiutl population decreased, the power source for the Kwakiutl political system (the potlatch) became more open, allowing more people to gain political power

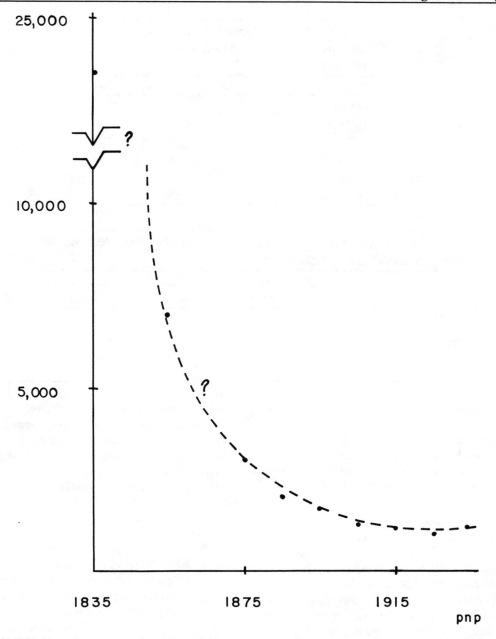

Figure 3.10. Kwakiutl population decline from contact to 1934 (adapted from Codere 1950:52).

(and hence deflating the power of existing leaders). With these changes the potlatch also became much more competitive. In Piddocke's (1969:153) words

> In post-contact times we find...an influx of new wealth...and a drastic decline in popu-lation....The result was...an increase in the size and frequency of potlatches, a general spread of potlatching to most persons in the Kwakiutl communities, [and] an increase in rivalrous potlatches with a

concomitant individualizing of potlatches (1969:153).

Kiriwina Island and the Kula Ring

The second case of change in a prestige-good system comes from Melanesia. The Trobriand Islands are situated just off the southeast coast of New Guinea. There are three main islands in the Trobriands: Kitava, Vakua, and Kiriwina. Kiriwina Island itself is divided into six districts, and it is the

Table 3.1. Largest Potlatches Between 1849 and 1949 (adapted from Codere 1950:94).

Dates	No. of Blankets
before 1849	320
1849-1869	9,000
1870-1889	7,000
1890-1909	18,000
1910-1929	14,000
1930-1949	33,000

Table 3.2. The Number of Large Potlatches Given Between 1850 and 1940 (adapted from Codere 1950:96).

Date	Over 5,000 Blankets	Over 10,000 Blankets	Over 20,000 Blankets
1850-1874	1		
1875-1899	3	3	
1900-1924		2	
1925-1940			2

northernmost district, also called Kiriwina, that I focus on.

The Trobriands are perhaps best known for their participation in the Kula ring, described by Bronislaw Malinowski in a 1920 article in *Man*, and more fully in his 1922 classic *Argonauts of the Western Pacific*. Put concisely, the Kula

> is a form of exchange, of extensive, inter-tribal character; it is carried on by communities inhabiting a wide ring of islands, which form a closed circuit.... Along this route articles of two kinds, and two kinds only, are constantly traveling in opposite directions. In the direction of the hands of the clock, moves constantly...long necklaces of red shell...In the opposite direction moves...bracelets of white shell....Each of these articles, as it travels in its own direction on the closed circuit, meets on its way articles of the other class, and is constantly being exchanged for them. Every movement of the Kula articles, every detail of the transactions is fixed and regulated by a set of traditional rules and conventions... (Malinowski 1922:81).

The Kula articles themselves are quite simple: shell necklaces and arm-bracelets. They are considered to be ornaments, but are rarely worn (Malinowski 1922:87-88). Malinowski (1922:89) compares the Kula articles to the Crown Jewels because both are "too valuable and too cumbersome to be worn...ownership of them with the ensuing renown is the main source of their value. Also both...are cherished because of the historical sentiment which surrounds them." Truly renowned Kula articles will have individual names and histories, and are recognized by all the people of the Kula ring.

The Kula ring itself extends from the Kiriwina in the north to Wari in the south, and from Murua in the east to Goodenough in the west. The probable trade routes in the ring are given in Figure 3.11. The Kula ring, as suggested by Figure 3.11 is a very complex exchange system, and Malinowski only saw a small portion of it (Brunton 1975:545-547). Many goods are exchanged in other parts of the ring, such as green-stone, boar's tusks, and different types of shell ornaments (Brunton 1975:546-47), and behaviors associated with the Kula are as varied as these goods. Indeed, Annette Weiner (1976, 1989) has shown that there is a separate but equally complex system of womens' exchanges that Malinowski (and others) completely missed. In short, understanding the entire Kula ring and all its variations would be an immense (and fascinating) undertaking, but Malinowski's description of the Kula in the Trobriands, albeit simplistic, should be adequate for my purposes.

Kula exchanges in the Trobriands are conducted between formal trade partners. Malinowski (1922:85)

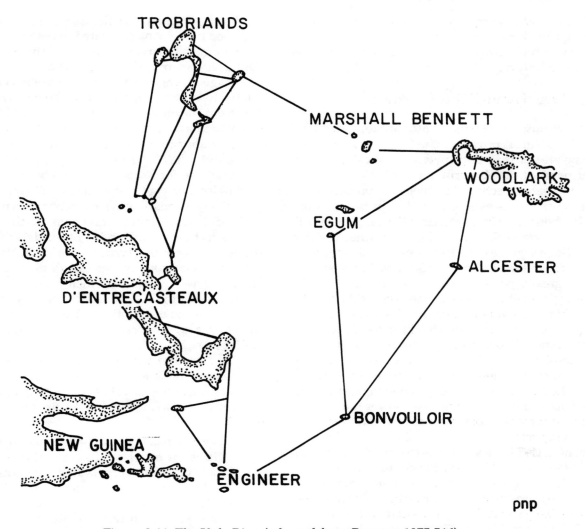

TROBRIANDS

MARSHALL BENNETT

WOODLARK

EGUM

ALCESTER

D'ENTRECASTEAUX

BONVOULOIR

NEW GUINEA

ENGINEER

pnp

Figure 3.11. The Kula Ring (adapted from Brunton 1975:546).

tells us "This partnership is a lifelong relationship, it implies various mutual duties and privileges, and constitutes a type of inter-tribal relationship on an enormous scale." Each person who participates in the Kula must have at least two trade partners, one clockwise and one counterclockwise, but there is no limit to the number one can have. An ordinary Trobriand Islander will Kula with the nearby village chiefs, and perhaps one or two other people in those villages. However, Malinowski (1922:91) tells us that village chiefs may have hundreds of Kula partners.

The Kula ring obviously functioned as a prestige-good system, and indeed John Persson (1983:44-45) has defined it as one. Power was associated with the number of Kula partners one had. As Ron Brunton (1975:553) tells us "Participation in the kula became the basis of social differentiation with political success based largely on success in the kula." Since only one prestige-good comes from each partner, political

power is more simply associated with the control of large numbers of imported prestige-goods. The Kula is a formal structure through which prestige-goods are moved, and it is a means to gain political power through the control of imported prestige-goods.

The power of chiefs in the northern Trobriands was unique in the Kula ring: "Northern Kiriwina in particular...is generally regarded as anomalous as far as ranked clans and hereditary elite are concerned" (Persson 1983:33). Brunton (1975:544) echoes this statement:

the Trobriand political system differs from the usual Melanesian Big-man type, both in the ascription of differential rank to the sub-clans (dala), which operates to limit eligibility for leadership, and the extent to which the status of leader is recognized and given legitimacy.

In the northern Trobriands, chiefs came from high-ranking sub-clans in an ascribed hierarchy, and their power was much greater than other political leaders within the Kula ring.

Trade Density and Chiefly Power

Both Brunton and Persson attempt to understand how the political power of chiefs in the Trobriands became greater than the power of political leaders in other parts of the Kula ring. The conclusions they come to relate directly to the theory of prestige-good system process I developed earlier in this chapter. Indeed, both relate heightened political power with decreasing trade density, although neither use that term. Their argument is that a periodic lack of prestige-goods in the northern Trobriands offers political leaders greater political power. As Persson (1983:38) explains "A limited supply of valuables will stimulate hierarchization, whereas their overflow will frustrate this process and turn it in the direction of political disintegration." This is exactly like the case in Figure 3.6 where there is a stable population and a decrease in the flow of prestige-goods. According to my theory of social evolution in prestige-good systems, this situation should result in increasing power for political leaders, and this is exactly what both Brunton and Persson suggest.

Brunton (1975:544-45) argues that the physical location of the northern Trobriands with respect to the rest of the Kula ring "afforded greater potential for individual or group control over crucial political resources [i.e. prestige-goods] than elsewhere in the Massim area." Brunton (1975:547-48) simply claims that Kiriwina "is in a rather precarious position in the kula network," because it has to compete with three other areas in getting access to Kula goods (see Figure 3.12).

Brunton offers three sources of evidence for Kiriwina's precarious position in the Kula ring. First, there is physical evidence from the number of goods that pass through the Kiriwina district: "out of 707 armshells passing through the Trobriands...Kiriwina was able to get less than a third" (Brunton 1975:549). Second, there is indirect evidence from the nature of trade partnerships. In most parts of the Kula ring, trade partnership is a flexible arrangement. If a trade partner becomes ungenerous or disengaged with the Kula ring, the partnership is easily terminated. This is not true in Kiriwina, where trade partnerships are considered lifelong relationships (recall Malinowski's statement above). Brunton (1975:549) argues that Kiriwina's emphasis on lifelong trade partnerships stems from their precarious position in the Kula ring—partnerships are maintained at all costs in order to maintain already limited access to Kula goods.

Finally, Brunton also discusses the way Kula goods are used in Kiriwina compared to the way other areas use them as indirect evidence of their scarcity. In Dobu, for example, Kula goods are necessities for marriage arrangements, and are often saved up for years to make a particularly large bridewealth payment (Brunton 1975:549). In Kitava, Kula articles are also saved up for long periods of time in order to make elaborate funerary distributions (Brunton 1975:549). The Kiriwinans, on the other hand, have minimal use for Kula articles in non-Kula contexts, and indeed attempt to pass them on to trade partners as quickly as possible after receiving them (Brunton 1975:550). This again is in response to the scarcity of goods in Kiriwina. Goods are needed to maintain trade partnerships and access to the Kula ring. The Kiriwinans do not have the luxury to store up goods, because few come through their hands. If they stored Kula goods up, they would lose trade partners who would become disgruntled at having to wait, perhaps many years, for a reciprocal exchange (Brunton 1975:549).

The fact that Kiriwinans do not manufacture anything of value to other Massim societies combines with the scarcity of Kula goods to give increased power to Kiriwinan chiefs. As Brunton (1975:554) explains:

> In Kiriwina...the entrepreneurial opportunities for other men to exploit through trade etc. were very limited...the presence and elaboration of chieftainship and rank in the Northern Trobriands can best be understood in terms of factors which permitted the development of a more controlled exchange system than existed elsewhere. The opportunities available for ambitious men to create a "fund of power" and strike out on their own were restricted.

In summary, Brunton (1975:554-56) makes this statement concerning the development of ranked sub-clan hierarchies and powerful chiefs in the northern Trobriands:

> Trobriand chieftainship resulted...from a scarcity of valuables. This scarcity was not simply a result of population density but was a consequence of the operation of external exchange networks and the distribution of non-agricultural resources. The reason why "both the principle of rank and the power of the chief break down more and more as we move south" (Malinowski 1922:69), is that communities in the south were better placed in terms of their access

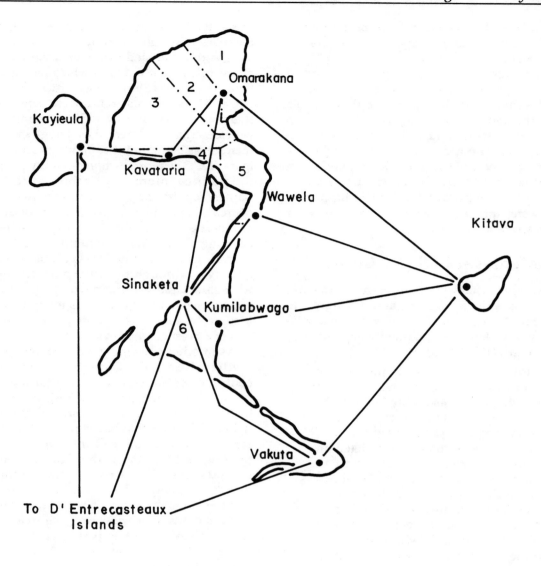

pnp

Figure 3.12. Kula routes in the Trobriands (adapted from Brunton 1975:548). Numbers 1-6 are districts on Kiriwina Island; number 1 is Kiriwina district itself.

to the kula and other important resources. Monopolization of political tokens by individuals or groups was therefore less possible....Given the fundamental importance of exchange in Melanesian politics, we must...examine whether the main wealth items can be controlled...if we are to understand the origins of hereditary social stratification and chieftainship.

Persson (1983:40) makes a similar argument, but in more general terms:

A position in the mainstream of the flow of goods brings about an *egalitarian* local structure. The function of the valuables as a basis for the growth and rank of an elite group is undermined as their abundance does not allow exclusive control. A position at the periphery of exchanges, on the contrary, generates a *hierarchical* local structure. Thanks to their scarcity, the goods may be monopolized to serve as a chiefly fund of power.

Persson (1983:42-44) also make the important point that Kiriwina was able to intensify production for the support of chiefs.

These arguments closely parallel the theory of social evolution in prestige-good systems I presented earlier in this chapter. With a stable population and a decrease in the trade density, the power of Kiriwinan chiefs grew. Other areas of the Kula ring did not experience this growth of power, but did not face the low trade density or competition for Kula goods that Kiriwina did. And Kiriwina had the potential to increase subsistence production for the support of chiefs and were, apparently, willing to do so in order to maintain access to kula goods.

The Medieval Catholic Church

The third case of change in prestige-good systems I want to discuss is the Medieval Catholic Church. In the central Middle Ages, the Church was both a political and economic body, as eloquently explained by Richard Southern (1970:24-25):

> The Middle Ages may be defined as the period in western European history when the church could reasonably claim to be one true state, and when men (however much they might differ about the nature of ecclesiastical and secular power) acted on the assumption that the church had an overriding political authority...Hobbes's gibe about the papacy being the ghost of the Roman Empire sitting crowned upon the grave thereof has a greater truth than he realized...During the whole medieval period there was in Rome a single spiritual and temporal authority exercising powers which in the end exceeded those that had ever lain within the grasp of the Roman Emperor.

Holy relics were central to the Church in the Middle Ages, for relics were the basis of political and economic power. And because relics were the basis of power, the Medieval Church offers an interesting (perhaps extreme) example of a prestige-good system.

In Chapter 2, I stated that prestige-good systems have the following structures: (1) generalized exchange of prestige-goods; (2) control over prestige-goods at the highest political level; (3) the reproduction of basic kinship structures in the political structure; and (4) political power held by the socially eldest members of society. The Medieval Catholic Church contained all these structures. Generalized exchange in holy relics was widespread, as I will discuss below. Monopoly over these relics

was at the highest level. It can be argued, indeed, that the relics were controlled by the saints themselves (at least within the Medieval world view). No one had access to a relic if the saint who's relic it was did not want the individual to have it. As Patrick Geary (1978:152-53) tells us "relics were actually the saints themselves, continuing to live among men...relics were described and treated as though they were saints themselves living in the community and participating in its life." The reproduction of family relationships in the political hierarchy of the Church is obvious (father/son, brother/sister, and the like). Finally, the church's hierarchy was made up of social elders. Just as Meillassoux described for African "self-sustaining" economies, in order to gain power in the Medieval Catholic Church one had to reproduce the social order by moving through the ritual grades, allying oneself with elders and gaining power from them (through appointments to higher levels in the hierarchy). The Medieval Catholic Church fits well within the definition of a prestige-good system.

As in other prestige-good systems, power in the Medieval Catholic Church was based upon the control of prestige-goods in the form of holy relics. There were three classes of relics: (1) parts of the bodies of saints and the instruments of Christ's crucifixion; (2) objects that had come in close contact with saints, such as clothing or instruments of a martyr's torture; and (3) objects that had touched first and second class relics (Cruz 1984:2). In the Medieval world view, holy relics, particularly of the first class, had tremendous power. They could perform miracles and bring divine providence to the area in which they were located, benefiting perhaps entire communities (Geary 1978:37-40). Southern (1970:31) describes holy relics in this way:

> Relics were the main channel through which supernatural power was available for the needs of ordinary life. Ordinary men could see and handle them, yet they belonged not to this transitory world but to eternity. On the Last Day they would be claimed by the saints and become an integral part of the kingdom of Heaven. Among all the objects of the visible, malign, unintelligible world, relics alone were both visible and full of beneficent intelligence.

As explained above, the Medieval individual saw relics not as the remains of saints, but as the saints themselves. By having saintly relics in one's possession, one also had the saint in one's possession (more accurately, the saint had the possessor of the relic in his service). Nowhere is this made more plain than in the nature of the papacy. The pope was (and still is) "The Vicar of St. Peter." In the Medieval Church this title was taken quite literally. The pope spoke for St. Peter, as Southern (1970:30) explains:

> the pope, whatever theoretical claims were made for him, in practice owed most of his authority to the fact that he was the guardian of the body of St. Peter. This brought men to Rome and made them listen to the voice of St. Peter mediated through his representative on earth.

Southern (1970:94-95) later expands this point:

> For the western church from the seventh to the eleventh century the existence of the tomb of St. Peter was the most significant fact in Christendom. The body within the tomb, which would one day clothe the door-keeper of heaven, was the link between the presence in heaven and the church on earth....The rulers and pilgrims from the newly converted peoples of Europe, who came to Rome to be baptized and if possible to die in the presence of the Apostle, were not drawn by any sophisticated theories of papal authority but by the conviction that they could nowhere find such safety as in the physical presence of the keeper of the keys of heaven.

> St. Peter still worked in the tomb, but his *persona* on earth was entrusted to the pope. Therefore, although men came to Rome in the first place to visit the Apostle, they prostrated themselves before the pope.

Just as the pope's power lay in the saintly relic he controlled (the body of St. Peter), so the power of churches and monasteries throughout Europe were based upon the relics they contained. Joan Cruz (1985:5) explains that "When the cult of relics came to its full height during the Middle Ages, many great churches owed their sanctity and renown simply to the presence of important relics." Economic power also flowed from the saintly relics. Renowned relics brought pilgrims, and pilgrims brought tithes and alms. Funds for special projects were generated by carrying saintly relics around the countryside and asking for donations (Geary 1978:76). As Geary (1978:69) explains:

> the monasteries had few resources to meet the challenges of...[their] precarious existence. Lacking human protection in the forms of military or economic force, they

looked to the protection of saints to reestablish lost prestige, intimidate local magnates, and outdistance other monasteries in the race for spiritual renown.

Cities found these same benefits in holy relics, and sought for their churches to have them: "the presence of a widely honored saint could provide the means of establishing or maintaining economic power and a competitive position vis-a-vis other cities" (Geary 1978:107).

Churches and monasteries needed relics more than simply for the renown and power they brought; after the year 801 they needed them physically to continue as places of worship. The Council of Carthage required that all altars contain relics (Geary 1978:20,42). The ramifications of this for the social reproduction of the Catholic community is obvious. If one did not have a relic, one did not have a place of worship. For the burgeoning population of Catholics this was a major problem. Travel in Medieval Europe was extremely difficult (see d'Haucourt 1963:19-23), so what was one to do for marriage and burial rites if the local church or monastery no longer had a "functioning" altar?

Relics and the Growth of Power

Charlemagne was crucial in increasing the power and importance of holy relics in Medieval Europe. He not only encouraged the destruction of altars that did not contain relics, but encouraged the use of relics in social and legal situations. In the year 803 he made it imperative that oaths be sworn either in a church or upon a holy relic (Geary 1978:43-44). At this same time, sainthood and associated relics began to be regulated by the Church. The Synod of Frankfort declared in the year 794 "that no new saints be venerated or invoked...but only those who were chosen by the authority of their passion or by the merit of their life are to be venerated in church" (quoted in Geary 1978:45). In addition to this, martyrdom (in Europe at least) had all but disappeared. The result was that few new holy relics were available at a time when they were in great demand by the burgeoning Catholic populace of Europe: "With the foundation of new monasteries, the beginnings of the establishment of a system of parishes, and the reform of places of worship that had fallen into disuse, the demand for acceptable relics must have greatly exceeded the supply" (Geary 1978:45).

With the Medieval Catholic Church one has the situation of a prestige-good system with a steady (or slightly declining) flow of prestige-goods and a growing population. According to the theory of prestige-good system evolution I developed earlier, this situation should result in a decrease in trade density, conflict over the goods that are available, and an increase in the power of those who control prestige-goods. In the particular case of the Medieval Catholic Church, this situation should result in conflict over holy relics, and an increase in the power and importance of churches and monasteries that controlled important relics.

In terms of conflict, the case is very clear. It was precisely at this time that *furta sacra*, the theft of holy relics, became widespread. In his fascinating book on the subject, Patrick Geary (1978) offers six reasons for the stealing of relics, all of which support the notion that conflict over these relics was intense. The first reason was for the creation of a new religious organization. Geary (1978:158) explains that "As religious communities developed, as parishes were established and populations increased, this basic need [for relics] continued to be felt." The second reason was to obtain relics of a particular organization's patron. Geary (1978:159) tells us "devotion to a saint over a period of time in a particular location tended to produce the physical remains of the saint." The third reason was to gain the protective powers of a powerful saint in a time of political turmoil (Geary 1978:159). The fourth reason was to gain prestige for one's organization or community (Geary 1978:159). The fifth reason was to make one's organization or community more popular by acquiring the remains of a popular saint (Geary 1978:159). Finally, the sixth reason for stealing relics was that "the possession of really important relics could compensate for defects in other areas" (Geary 1978:159). Indeed, conflict over relics was so great at this time that Geary tells us "Possession of stolen relics came to be regarded as a mark of prestige in itself" (Geary 1978:160), partially because this showed the power of the organization in being able to successfully outcompete rivals for relics.

In terms of growing power associated with the control of important relics, the case is equally clear. Geary (1978:107) discusses at length several cases where Italian towns worked to acquire important relics in order to bolster their power and ensure their continued existence. As he (Geary 1978:107) tells us "These towns were struggling toward autonomy, both from the Byzantine Empire and...from the Carolingians...the presence of a widely honored saint could provide the means of establishing or maintaining economic power and a competitive position." Geary (1978:110-11) explains in more detail that

> the importance of Apostolic sees was well established, and in Italy belief in the superiority of churches possessing the remains

of Apostles had a venerable tradition by the ninth century. Most obvious of course was the apostolic character of the Church of Rome with the tombs of Peter and Paul. But since the time of Saint Ambrose, northern Italian towns which could not claim Apostolic foundation for their churches had been carefully acquiring relics of apostles for religious and political reasons.

Venice was one of the northern towns that stole the remains of an apostle for the political power it brought. Venice chose to steal St. Mark from Alexandria, not only because of the prestige it could bring, but more importantly because St. Mark had been an Italian evangelist. The decision to steal St. Mark "was clearly a step away from Byzantine influence in the city" (Geary 1978:111). In stealing the body of this saint, the Venicians hoped to bolster their position in respect to both the Byzantines and their rival cities in Italy. As Geary (1978:115) makes clear

> There is little doubt of the ultimate success of the venture...Venice accomplished, with the help of her new patron, exactly what she had set out to do: achieve superiority over the towns of the northern coast of the Adriatic, and independence from her Byzantine "masters."

Venice is a clear example of power growing through the control of important relics during the central Middle Ages.

The Medieval Catholic Church appears to support my theory of social evolution in prestige-good systems. When the trade density of holy relics decreased because of an expanding population, competition erupted over the control of relics, culminating in the tradition of *furta sacra*. Those who came to control important relics, such as the city of Venice, gained tremendous power through their acquisition. Indeed, this is a time when the power of Rome and the papacy were growing, and as Geary and Southern suggest, this may have been in part because of the presence of St. Peter's tomb.

Conclusions

The three prestige-good systems I discussed in this chapter all support my theory of social evolution in prestige-good systems. Political power in prestige-good systems appears to be a function of trade density. When trade density increases, the potential power of political leaders decreases. When trade density decreases, the potential power of political leaders increases. Of course, the ability of political leaders to increase their power is dependent on numerous other factors, not the least of which is the society's ability to intensify subsistence production to support them.

It is important to note that this theory only suggests potential changes in political power, and is not meant to be a causal model. Increasing trade density does not necessarily cause the power of political leaders in prestige-good systems to decline, it merely undermines their traditional power base. These leaders may be able to build another power base and maintain their power. In the same vein, just because trade density decreases does not necessarily mean that a despotic ruler will emerge. As stated above, inability to increase subsistence production may stifle any increase in political power, and other variables may work to decrease a potential despotic ruler's power.

In short, this theory of social evolution in prestige-good systems is not a causal one. It appears, from the societies that I and others (Salisbury 1962; Friedman 1982) have considered, that changes in trade density foster changes in political power within prestige-good systems. This makes sense given the nature of political power in prestige-good systems, but it does not mean that political leaders will not find new power sources if others dry up, or that their power will not change in the absence of change in trade density. Still, trade density appears to be strongly correlated with political power in prestige-good systems, and change in trade density with change in political power.

Finally, it should be noted that I have only considered one aspect of social evolution in this chapter: change in the power of political leaders. This sort of change can, however, bring in its wake a myriad of other social changes in scale, integration, and complexity. For example, the intensification of subsistence production needed to support emergent political centralization might foster the development of a new transport system, and hence increase integration within the society. So while I have only considered change in political power, the effects of change in political power are often pan-societal.

Some Propositions on the Evolution of Prestige-Good Systems

Having considered the nature of prestige-good systems and evolution within prestige-good systems, I want to give some thought to the evolution of prestige-good systems themselves. Although a lack of solid supporting evidence may make this discussion seem little more than a "just-so" story, I think it serves well as an expanded look at the nature of political

power in prestige-good systems, and as a reiteration of the major points made in the last two chapters.

In order to consider the evolution of prestige-good systems, it is essential to recognize that in prestige-good systems political leaders do not control the means of production. Individuals in the societies considered in this and the last chapter were able to provide for themselves without the aid or approval of political leaders. Kongo is a good example. Although the King was considered the ultimate owner of all land, Ekholm (1972:83) makes it clear that his ownership was purely symbolic, and that he held no coercive power over the Kongan people in this respect:

> The king's "right of ownership" of land was in the category of religion and politics: it involved no effective control over land...he could not deprive anyone of his right to cultivate the land....Neither did the king's "ownership" of land give him the right to what was produced.

While individuals have no problems providing subsistence for themselves in prestige-good systems, they are unable to provide themselves with exotic goods and esoteric knowledge necessary to maintain or increase their social position. For this they need the assistance or approval of a political leader. In prestige-good systems political power stems not from the control of the means of production, but from the control of the means of social reproduction. As Meillassoux (1978:36-37) suggests, controlling the means of social reproduction is an alternative strategy for gaining political power in situations were controlling the means of production is difficult or impossible:

> The fact that the means of production observed in these societies [with traditional economies] are simple and accessible means that they cannot be used as a means for controlling the producers...The fact that at this stage it is impossible to control the means of production effectively and therefore impossible to control the producer through them, makes control over the producer himself essential, by the development of prior relations of a personal rather than a material nature.

This leads to my first proposition on the evolution of prestige-good systems: prestige-good systems evolve in situations where gaining control over the means of production is difficult, but where gaining control over the means (or a means) of social reproduction is comparatively easy.

In many situations, control of the means of social reproduction may already be held by persons with specific social roles, such as lineage elders. If the control over the means of social reproduction is already socially legitimated, then emergent political leaders should find it useful to employ the existing framework of legitimation to legitimize their own emerging power (Meillassoux 1978:146-49). This leads to my second proposition on the evolution of prestige-good systems: prestige-good systems evolve in situations where there are existing social positions whose members control (at least in part) the means of social reproduction. Emergent political leaders are then able to place themselves in these social positions while converting them into political positions, hence legitimizing the new political structure through the existing social structure. This explains the tendency I have pointed out for social relationships to be reproduced in the political hierarchy of prestige-good systems.

A final proposition on the evolution of prestige-good systems comes from the basic necessity of political leaders to maintain absolute control over prestige-goods entering and moving through the system. Prestige-good systems must evolve in situations where societies are relatively bounded (in terms of mobility), and in the absence of an open market system. Either of these elements could severely restrict an emergent leader's ability to control the influx and distribution of prestige-goods (Ekholm 1977:130-131).

The six societies considered so far share these three elements. Their political leaders do not control the means of production. There are social positions (elders, ritual grades, and the like) in which members control certain exotic goods or esoteric knowledge, and these social positions are reproduced in the political hierarchy. They are all relatively bounded, and none has a market system through which prestige-goods pass.

It is unfortunate that none of these six societies have archaeological sequences that are known well enough to test the ideas about the evolution of prestige-good systems I have presented here. Tonga perhaps comes closest. The Tongan prestige-good system evolved in an obviously bounded situation, and where the means of production (rainfall horticulture with domestic animals, gathering, and fishing) would have been difficult to control on the numerous arable islands in the archipelago (see Davidson 1979). There is also some evidence for the existence of positions like that of lineage elder or head in the social structure of the prehistoric inhabitants of Tonga (Kirch 1984:31-40, 62-69, 223). But even this archaeological sequence is based upon sketchy and incomplete data from a very few excavations in the archipelago, and is certainly not sufficient to fully evaluate these ideas.

4

Prestige-Goods

In this chapter I develop categories of prestige-goods from ethnographic contexts to compare with the material record for the Mississippian period. I develop these categories through both descriptive and statistical analyses of prestige-goods used in ethnographically-known societies that are either prestige-good systems or have leadership positions where control of such goods is an important element in gaining and maintaining power. I also consider the social relationships surrounding the use of prestige-goods in these societies. Their locations in communities, their tendency to be placed in burials, their use by one sex or another, and the like, may reflect the way prestige-goods were used by the Mississippian peoples, and may help generate hypotheses concerning the locations and contexts in which one might find Mississippian prestige-goods.

The Sample

The societies I chose for these analyses come from the Standard Cross-Cultural Sample (Murdock and White 1969). I selected those societies in the Sample that appeared to be politically and economically similar to the prestige-good systems described in the previous chapters using the coded variables and data sets available in Volume Five of the *World Cultures Journal of Comparative and Cross-Cultural Research*. The variables I used were numbers 1 (Intercommunity trade as food source), 2 (Food import acquisition), 17 (Money), 20 (Food storage), 155 (Cultural complexity scale #7—Money), and 574 (Achieved leadership through wealth distribution). Definitions and values for these variables are presented in Table 4.1.

I dropped societies from the sample if the society had no intercommunity trade in food (Variable 1, value 1). Intercommunity trade, as explained in the previous chapters, is crucial to the functioning of a prestige-good system, for it is only through the control of prestige-goods, often imported from other polities, that political leaders are able to maintain power in these systems. Although this variable is stated as specific to trade in food only, the variable coded with a value of 1 suggests that there is no inter-community trade of any sort. Indeed, in most cases of intercommunity trade (the Kula for example), food items accompany prestige-goods, and vice-versa. Culling on this variable removed seven societies from the sample.

I next culled societies from the sample if they had markets (Variable 2, value 3). As explained in the last chapter, the presence of markets makes the maintenance of a prestige-good system difficult because markets potentially allow for the open sale of prestige-goods. Again, this variable is directed only at food items, but the presence of a market system allows the possibility of open trade in prestige-goods, so the 28 societies coded as having food markets were also removed from the sample.

I used variables 17 and 155 to eliminate societies with indigenous or external currency from the sample (Variable 17, values 4 and 5; Variable 155, values 3 and 5). The presence of indigenous currency suggests that political leaders have the potential to manipulate the total economy by manipulating money supplies, and not simply prestige-goods flowing through it. Although this can be an important strategy for gaining political power, it is not the strategy employed in prestige-good systems. Similarly, the presence of foreign currency in a society suggests the presence of foreign political power. Certainly some foreign polity has influence over the society's economy if their currency is being used. The presence of foreign influence over the economy suggests that indigenous political leaders might have to seek alternative strategies to maintain their own positions, and

Table 4.1. Variables Used in Selecting Societies From the Standard Cross-Cultural Sample that are Structurally Similar to Known Prestige-Good Systems.

Variable 1: Intercommunity Trade as Food Source
1 = no trade
2 = food imports absent although trade present
3 = trade in salt and minerals only
4 = < 10% of food from trade
5 = > 10% of food from trade, but less than any single local source
6 = < 50% of food from trade, and more than any single local source
7 = > 50% of food from trade

Variable 2: Food Import Acquisition
1 = direct individual exchanges
2 = indirect individual exchanges
3 = local markets
4 = middlemen
5 = three or four of above

Variable 17: Money (Media of Exchange) and Credit
1 = no media of exchange or money
2 = domestically usable articles as media of exchange
3 = tokens of conventional value as media of exchange
4 = foreign coinage or paper currency
5 = indigenous coinage or paper currency

Variable 20: Food Storage
1 = none
2 = individual households
3 = communal facilities
4 = political agent controlled repositories
5 = economic agent controlled repositories

Variable 155: Cultural Complexity Scale #7 - Money
1 = none
2 = domestically usable articles
3 = alien currency
4 = elementary forms
5 = true money

Variable 574: Achieved Leadership Through Wealth Distribution
1 = acts of wealth distribution which bring prestige to the giver are not one of the most important
    factors in attaining and maintaining the highest degree of political power in the society
2 = acts of wealth distribution which bring prestige to the giver are one of the most important factors
    in attaining and maintaining the highest degree of political power in the society

although these might rest in part on the control of prestige-goods, the situation would be much more complex than the kind of prestige-good system I am researching. In addition, the presence of true, completely fungible currency implies the presence of a market economy. This is in total opposition to the functioning of a prestige-good system, where pres-

tige-goods must be kept out of general circulation. The presence of foreign or indigenous currency, then, is inconsistent with the functioning of a prestige-good system, and I dropped those societies which had either. I used both Variables 17 and 155 to cull the sample because several societies coded as having missing data for Variable 17 had data coded for

Variable 155. In all I dropped fifty-five societies from the sample based on these two variables.

Variable 20 allowed me to eliminate those societies which had political or economic agents controlling food stores (values 4 and 5). Control of food stores suggests a method of controlling an economy in a much more direct way than in a prestige-good system. The political strategy employed in this case is more complex than that of the simple prestige-good systems I wanted to use for this study. Actually, Variable 20 eliminated only two societies from the sample, the Aztecs and the Incas. Although the political strategies of the Aztecs were oriented in many ways to the control of prestige-goods, they employed a more complex and broader means of control than that of a simple prestige-good system. Indeed Richard Blanton (n.d.) has recently argued that manipulation of the market system, in addition to the control of goods flowing through them (as one would expect in a prestige-good system), was a basic strategy of Aztec empire building. Although the same might not be true of the Incas, both societies functioned through more complex political strategies than simple prestige-good systems, and should be removed from the sample.

Finally, I used Variable 574 to eliminate societies in which the distribution of wealth to gain prestige, if present, was not an important means of achieving and maintaining political power (value 1). This is obviously in opposition to the basic political structure of a prestige-good system. Thirty societies were dropped from the sample on this variable.

In all, sixty-four societies survived the culling. I consulted basic ethnographic works on these societies following the Bibliography for the Standard Cross-Cultural Sample given in Volume 2, number 1 of *World Cultures*. Upon reading the ethnographic works for these societies it became apparent that the control of goods was not an important political strategy in some of the societies that survived the culling. Although they were consistent with prestige-good systems in terms of the variables considered, they were not at all like prestige-good systems in terms of political strategies.

I also found that a number of pastoral societies had survived the culling. These are problematic, as the main source of wealth is animals, and these animals are also a primary food source. Political power based upon an individual's wealth in animals could be consistent with the nature of prestige-good systems, but if these animals are basic to subsistence, then this situation could also be seen as political power based upon an individual's control over the means of production. Control over the means of production is markedly inconsistent with the basic political strategy of prestige-good systems. In addition, pastoralists are often

market-oriented, or practice open trade with neighboring agriculturalists. This suggests that pastoralists are generally part of a market or open trading economy, and this is also inconsistent with the basic nature of prestige-good systems. Because of these problems I decided to drop pastoralists from the sample.

I also decided that before coding prestige-goods, I should read through the ethnographic literature for the non-pastoralist societies in the sample, and conduct yet another culling. In this culling I removed societies in which the control of wealth was not an important political strategy. This final culling brought the sample down to twenty-seven societies. Their names are given in Table 4.2. Brief descriptions of these societies are offered as Appendix B.

I need to make a few comments about the sample. I devised the culling strategy in order to make societies

Table 4.2. Twenty-Seven Societies From the Standard Cross-Cultural Sample Used in the Prestige-Goods Study.

Lozi
Mbundu
Kafa
Tiwi
New Ireland
Trobrianders
Siuai
Fijians
Ajie
Maori
Marquesans
Samoans
Atayal
Ingalik
Eyak
Haida
Twana
Yurok
Pomo
Klamath
Omaha
Huron
Creek
Apache
Bribri
Cubeo
Aymara

that were politically and economically inconsistent with prestige-good systems fall out easily, and to reduce the size of the sample to a manageable number. The culling was certainly not perfect, but followed a rational and defendable approach. The sample does not necessarily contain all the prestige-good systems that are part of the Standard Cross-Cultural Sample, but does contain those which I could most readily recognize. It is, in short, an opportunistic sample rather than a probabilistic one. In a similar vein, there is a great variety in the societies that survived the culling. Some are more obviously members of prestige-good systems, while others show only minimal signs. These twenty-seven societies are simply members of the Standard Cross-Cultural Sample that I was most easily able to recognize as having political and economic characteristics similar to the prestige-good systems I had already studied.

Coding Prestige-Goods

I considered objects to be prestige-goods and coded them if they: (1) were generally considered to be valuable, or served as a standard of value; (2) were symbols of status that were uniquely controlled by particular individuals or groups of individuals; or (3) were frequently used for brideprice, initiation, or funerary payments. The codebook I used is shown in Appendix A. The coded database itself can be found in Appendix B of Peregrine (1990). I must explain that the amount of information given about these types of goods varied widely in the ethnographic literature. Some societies had entire books written about their material culture, and some had lengthy ethnographies in which there was no mention of material goods. Because of this variability in data quality, I became concerned that the sample of prestige-goods might become heavily biased by societies for which I was able to find the most information.

I attempted to even out this variability by using the Human Relations Area Files when possible, and looking for prestige-goods under a standard set of codes. Unfortunately only sixteen of the twenty seven societies are included in HRAF. For these sixteen societies (see Appendix B for their names and brief descriptions), I searched the seven HRAF codes presented in Table 4.3 for mention of prestige-goods. Prestige-goods for the remaining eleven societies were gleaned from ethnographies. The data sources for these eleven societies are given next to their names in Appendix B, and a bibliography is also included.

The Average Prestige-Good

The average (modal) prestige-good is made from animal materials. It is a personal ornament of some kind, and is generally new. It is ovoid in form, white or silver in color, and has little decoration. It has a smooth finished surface, and is less than one cubic meter in size, frequently being less than ten cubic centimeters in size. The raw material, though local, requires high acquisition labor. Manufacturing labor is also high, but so is the object's durability. The object has an ordinary to extraordinary overall appearance.

There are few restrictions on the object's possession or use, although there is a trend for it to be used only by high-status males. While there may be no restrictions on the object's use, its possession is associated with social status. The object is often exchanged for a variety of goods or services that are generally of an equal or indeterminate value. Finally, the object is often placed in the grave of its possessor.

One can think of a variety of goods that might fit this "average" description. Animal teeth or claws, particularly strings of them, ivory and bone ornaments, such as labrets or earrings, shell beads or strings of shell beads all fit this description of an "average" prestige-good very well.

Table 4.3. HRAF Codes Used to Look for Prestige-Goods (after Murdock et al. 1982).	
436	Medium of Exchange: articles circulating in exchange at their intrinsic value as standard money.
554	Status, Role, and Prestige: symbolic tokens of the achievement of prestige; general statements on the various avenues of mobility.
556	Accumulation of Wealth: extent to which prestige can be gained through amassing or distributing wealth.
583	Mode of Marriage: wife-purchase; marriage by payment of consideration; marriage by gift exchange.
764	Funeral: burial rites; mortuary sacrifices; disposition of grave goods.
881	Puberty and Initiation: prevalence of special initiation rites for each sex; ceremonial sponsors.

Descriptive Analysis of the Prestige-Goods

Table 4.4 is a list of brief descriptions for the 132 coded prestige-goods. Glancing through this list, one can see that shell beads are quite common. Indeed, beads and strings of beads (shell and other) comprise 26 of the 132 goods, or almost 20% of the total sample. One might argue on the basis of this, and the description of the "average" prestige-good given above, that beads and strings of beads are a basic prestige-good in these systems.

A second and related third category of prestige-good, however, also becomes obvious when one looks over Table 4.4. Eleven of the goods listed, over 8% of the sample, are furs, while fourteen goods, about 11% of the total sample, are cloth or blankets. Together these two categories of cloth-like goods comprise about 19% of the total sample, nearly the same amount as bead goods.

On the surface these cloth-like objects do not seem to fit quite as well with the description of the "average" prestige-good given above, but some of the most obvious disparities can be readily explained. Cloth-like goods are certainly not personal ornaments, but the second and third most frequent class of object are utensils (cloth and blankets) and other (furs). Cloth-like goods are also not ovoid, but in terms of form rectanguloid (cloth and blankets) and other (furs) run a close second and third in frequency of occurrence. These goods are generally not white, but the second most frequent primary color is brown/tan, which matches the majority of furs and some of the cloth and blankets. Finally, these goods are not very durable, but moderate and high durability occur with nearly equal frequency in the sample.

A final category that seems obvious when looking over Table 4.4 is one of decorative status symbols, often made of precious metals. These are less obviously related to the "average" prestige-good described above, but evidence for a category of this type does seem apparent. There are 14 goods made of precious materials in the sample, and this third largest category of raw material type correlates well with a category of status goods. Many goods in this category would also be symbols of office, and hence some would likely be old. This fits with the second most frequent value in terms of age. Decorative status goods may also account for some of the heterogeneity in terms of color present in the sample, as well as much of the heterogeneity in terms of decoration. Neither shell goods nor cloth goods would have much decoration, so most of the coded decoration may come from status goods. They may also account for the large number of goods with an extraordinary appearance that are included in the sample.

Many of the restrictions coded in the sample may also be related to this category of status goods rather than the bead goods or cloth goods categories. In particular, the large number of goods that can be held only by political office personnel and those goods that have political significance in terms of social characteristics may be directly related to status goods. The modal frequency of goods being status symbols may also be related. In short, a category of decorative status symbols appears to be consistent with the "average" prestige-good when the variability inherent in the data is considered.

One can hypothesize, then, the existence of four basic categories of prestige-goods. The most obvious category is one consisting of bead goods. A second consists of cloth and blankets. A third category is comprised of furs. And a fourth is a heterogeneous category of status symbols, often decorative, colorful, and made of precious materials.

One can test for the presence or absence of these four hypothesized categories of prestige-goods by a variety of statistical methods, perhaps the most powerful being cluster analysis. Cluster analysis has the advantage over other potential methods (for example factor analysis or multidimensional scaling) of being relatively easy to interpret. It also allows for the rapid identification of clustered cases not originally hypothesized.

Cluster Analysis of the Prestige-Goods

Cluster analysis refers to a myriad of statistical methods and algorithms which can be used to find groups of cases that are related on a given set of variables (see Everitt 1974:1-5). The basic objective of cluster analysis is "to sort...observations into groups such that the degree of 'natural association' is high among members of the same group and low between members of different groups" (Anderberg 1973:3). This sorting can be done in a wide variety of ways.

Cluster analysis is carried out through three basic steps: (1) selecting the variables upon which to cluster cases; (2) selecting the clustering method or algorithm; and (3) interpreting the results (see Anderberg 1973:10-16). Selecting the variables in this case was rather easy. I considered only those variables that described the physical characteristics of the prestige-goods for use in the cluster analysis. These were PMT through APP. A large number of these variables had few respondents, and since an unknown on any of the variables used for the analysis would cause a case to be dropped, I used only variables with over 100 respondents. These variables were PMT, PMO, CLASS, FORM, PC, ACQ, MAN, DUR, and APP.

Table 4.4. Goods Coded for the Prestige-Goods Study.

0001-king's crown	0045-oval hatchet	0089-shell money
0002-gold ear-rings	0046-carved head	0090-trade beads (glass)
0003-gold armlet	0047-shell beads	0091-human scalp
0004-gold ring	0048-furs	0092-metal earplugs
0005-gold neck chain	0049-council sticks	0093-bracelet (gold,silver,copper)
0006-king's cloak	0050-dentalium shells	0094-moccasins
0007-silver staff	0051-wool blankets	0095-puberty clothes
0008-king's sword	0052-furs	0096-hide shield
0009-king's spear	0053-blankets	0097-buckskin
0010-king's gold shield	0054-skins	0098-abalone shell
0011-king's parasol	0055-armshells	0099-turquoise
0012-king's signal drum	0056-shell necklace	0100-feathers
0013-gold bracelet	0057-dentalium shells	0101-silver necklace
0014-royal drum	0058-clamshell beads	0102-seed necklace
0015-silver neck chain	0059-stone beads	0103-jaguar-tooth girdle
0016-governor's staff	0060-furs	0104-armadillo-vertebrae girdle
0017-red tunic	0061-plains-type clothes	0105-quartz-cylinder pendant
0018-leopard-skin tunic	0062-blankets	0106-pandanus mats
0019-red head-band	0063-beads (glass ?)	0107-tapa (barkcloth)
0020-chief's staff	0064-calico cloth	0108-black shell money
0021-silver neck chain	0065-leopard skin	0109-white shell money
0022-triple brass phallus	0066-eland-tail switch	0110-woodpecker scalps
0023-white turban	0067-national drums	0111-deerskin
0024-feather frontlet	0068-national spears	0112-obsidian blades
0025-hair comb	0069-king's pole	0113-shell discs
0026-tortoise-shell pin	0070-king's horn	0114-magnesite-cylinder beads
0027-pandanus mats	0071-rhinocerous-horn cane	0115-deerskin
0028-tapa (barkcloth)	0072-sub-chief's headdress	0116-red shell money
0029-whale's teeth	0073-cloth	0117-white shell money
0030-bone bracelet	0074-wax	0118-greenstone
0031-labret (wood)	0075-shells	0119-white heron feathers
0032-sea otter fur	0076-small shell beads	0120-shark's teeth
0033-Hudson's Bay blanket	0077-ostrich-eggshell beads	0121-whale's teeth
0034-copper shield	0078-salt	0122-greenstone pendant
0035-white shell money	0079-shell beads	0123-eagle feathers
0036-red shell money	0080-cotton cloth	0124-crow feathers
0037-slit gong	0081-labrets (bone)	0125-eagle war bonnet
0038-tanned skins	0082-gold "eagle"	0126-catlinite pipes with decorated stems
0039-pack-line bone	0083-red wood cane	0127-embroidered tobacco pouches
0040-dentalium shells	0084-shell money	0128-otter skins
0041-labrets (bone)	0085-woven cloth	0129-buffalo skins
0042-red ochre	0086-copper braclets	0130-embroidered clothes
0043-white shell money	0087-red cloth	0131-deer-tail headdress
0044-dark shell money	0088-embroidered headband	0132-ceremonial spears

Using these nine variables 90 valid cases were clustered.

I selected clustering methods following the suggestions given by Everitt (1974:7-41). Agglomerative hierarchical clustering techniques were the only ones I considered, as they are simple and powerful, and are perhaps the best suited to the type of analysis I wanted to perform (see Everitt 1974:92). These techniques agglomerate cases into a series of successively more inclusive groups, ending ultimately in a single group containing all cases. They begin by computing a distance matrix for all the cases. Cases or groups of cases are then successively fused to one another based upon their relative distances (Everitt 1974:8-9; Anderberg 1973:133). Cases become successively incorporated into larger and larger clusters until a single cluster of all cases is reached. The result is a dendrogram or tree showing the relative distances between cases through the location of branches which identify the successive fusions of cases and clusters.

Of the agglomerative hierarchical techniques available, the single linkage or nearest neighbor method is generally considered to be the best (Everitt 1974:62,92). The single linkage method proceeds by fusing cases and groups according to the distance between their nearest neighbors (Anderberg 1973:137-38). However, this method has a variety of problems associated with it, the most important being "chaining." Chaining refers to the fact that single linkage clustering tends to produce clusters of cases linked together by a chain of intermediate cases rather than homogeneous clusters with no intermediates (Everitt 1974:61), which can make interpretation difficult.

Centroid and Ward's methods of clustering tend to avoid the problem of chaining. The centroid method begins with the fusion of cases to form primary groups. These groups are then depicted as lying in Euclidean space, and defined by the coordinates of their centroid. Further fusion is based on the distances between group centroids (Everitt 1974:12-14). Ward's method attempts to minimize the loss of information about the cases being fused into clusters by using the sum of squared deviations of every case from the mean of the cluster to which the case belongs. Fusion of clusters proceeds by comparing every pair of clusters and fusing those whose combination results in the minimum increase in the sum of squared deviations (Everitt 1974:15-16).

I decided to use all three methods of clustering in the analysis, because each relies on different assumptions, different limitations, and has the potential of bringing out something different in the data (Everitt 1974:78-85). I performed the analyses themselves on the Purdue University Computing Center's IBM 3090 using the CLUSTER procedure in SPSSX (SPSS, Inc.

1988) with default settings (squared Euclidean distance as distance measurement). The dendrograms produced are given as Figures 4.1, 4.2, and 4.3

The Ward's method dendrogram (Figure 4.1) is perhaps the most easily interpretable of the three. The goods divide markedly into two groups between cases 99 and 105. The top group subdivides nicely between cases 78 and 100 into a cluster consisting of furs and other raw materials (1), and a cluster consisting of decorative clothing and clothing-like ornaments. Further subdivision of the second cluster between cases 98 and 95 creates a small cluster (with several outliers) of decorative clothes (3), and a heterogeneous cluster of personal ornaments (2).

The bottom group of the Ward's method dendrogram is much larger than the top, and seems to divide between cases 56 and 25. Again, the top cluster in this subdivision is large, and divides nicely between cases 10 and 28. The first cluster in this subdivision (4) consists of personal ornaments made from precious raw materials. The second cluster (5) is a heterogeneous group of personal ornaments, including many of the coded shell goods. The bottom cluster (6) in this subdivision cannot be divided easily. It is a heterogeneous group that does not seem to fit any clearly defined pattern in terms of the goods included, although the last few items seem to form a cluster of valuable exchange goods, including shell-money, copper shields, and obsidian blades.

The centroid method dendrogram (Figure 4.2) is also relatively easy to interpret, as the cases divided themselves well at the initial stage of analysis (which, of course, is one of the advantages of this method). The goods break down into two well-defined groups between cases 99 and 35. The top group seems to divide into three main clusters. The first (1) divides between cases 78 and 24, and consists of a heterogeneous group of personal ornaments and decorative clothes. The third cluster (3), which divides between cases 98 and 95, is made up of a similar group of heterogeneous personal ornaments.

In the bottom group of the centroid method dendrogram, a clean division can be made between cases 11 and 5. In the upper cluster of this subdivision, a further division can be made between cases 10 and 25. The top cluster here (4) consists of valuable exchange items, and one marked outlier (case 10). The bottom cluster (5) is made up of a very heterogeneous assortment of goods, mostly manufactured from natural materials. In the lower cluster of this subdivision, a further division can be made between cases 7 and 1. The top cluster of this subdivision (6) is composed of goods manufactured from precious materials, mainly personal ornaments. The bottom cluster (7) is another heterogeneous group of mainly

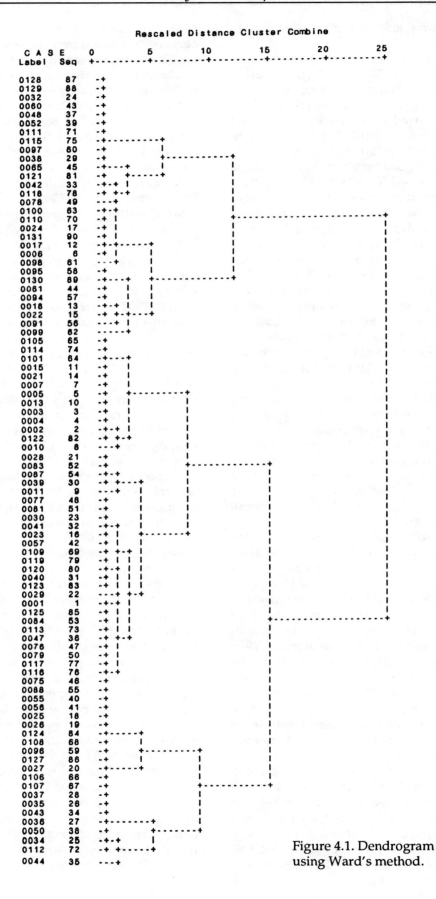

Figure 4.1. Dendrogram using Ward's method.

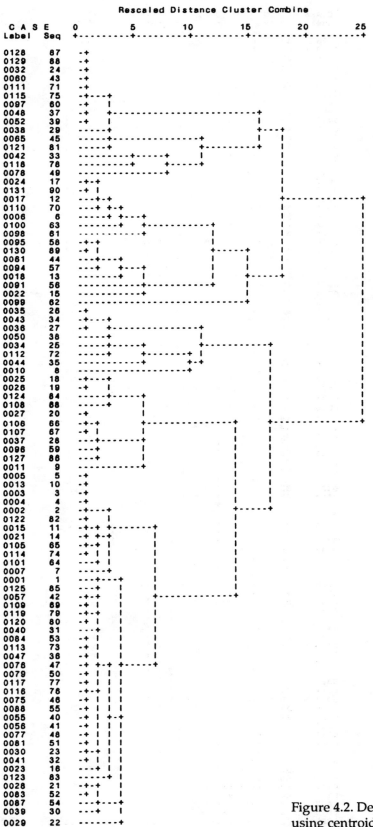

Figure 4.2. Dendrogram using centroid method.

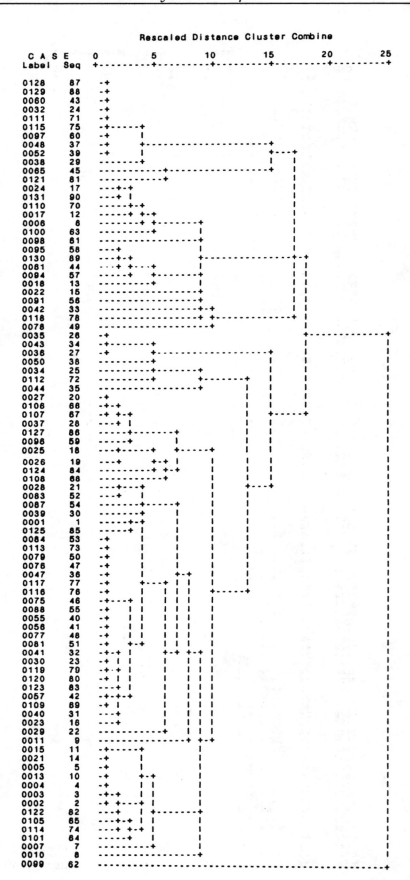

Figure 4.3.
Dendrogram using
single linkage method.

personal ornaments, including a tight grouping of shell goods in the center of the cluster.

The dendrogram produced using single linkage clustering (Figure 4.3) is not as easy to interpret as the other two as distances between clusters are not as marked, but a similar pattern of seven main clusters is apparent. The first cluster separates between cases 121 and 24. It consists mainly of furs. The second separates between cases 98 and 95, and consists of personal ornaments made of natural materials. The third cluster separates between cases 78 and 35. It is made up mainly of decorated clothing, but also contains a variety of raw materials. The fourth cluster separates between cases 44 and 27, and is made up of exchangeable valuables, mainly shell goods. The fifth cluster separates between cases 108 and 28, and consists of a very heterogeneous mixture of goods. The sixth separates between cases 11 and 15. It is composed of a variety of personal ornaments, with a tight grouping of shell goods. Finally, the seventh cluster consists mainly of goods manufactured from precious materials. One outlier (case 99) is not included in the analysis.

Several tight groupings are evident in the single linkage dendrogram. The first is in cluster 1, and includes the cases from 128 to 52. All these cases are furs. A second tight grouping can be seen in cluster 6. This grouping includes the 17 cases from 84 to 120. The majority of these cases are shell goods. The remainder are small goods made of bone or teeth, with one outlier (heron feathers, case 119). A third tight grouping is in cluster 7. This consists of seven personal ornaments made of precious metals, the cases between 15 and 2. Similar tight clusters can also be found in the centroid and Ward's method dendrograms.

The analyses of these dendrograms, then, supports the existence of three of the four hypothesized categories of prestige-goods: bead goods (particularly shell), furs, and heterogeneous status symbols (mainly personal ornaments). Cloth and blankets do not seem to form an obvious cluster, and indeed are mixed in throughout the clusters that are present. The analyses, while supporting the existence of these categories, also makes their description more complicated, as neither bead goods nor status symbols form tight clusters. There are also clusters of goods present in the dendrograms that do not fit well with the hypothesized categories.

A Second Cluster Analysis

In order to understand the nature of the diverse clusters uncovered in the previous analyses, I performed a different type of cluster analysis using the QUICK CLUSTER procedure in SPSSX (with default settings). QUICK CLUSTER employs the centroid method to cluster cases into a defined number of groups. Using this procedure I clustered the goods into 4, 5, 6, 7, 8, 9, and 10 groups. My analysis of the cluster memberships suggested that about seven distinct clusters are present in the data. Clustering based on less than seven groups tended to produce rather heterogeneous clusters. Clustering based on more than seven groups tended to produce clusters with very few cases, in some instances with only one member. Several groups also seemed to become relatively stable when the number of groups rose above six or seven. Case numbers and descriptions of the goods in each cluster are given in Table 4.5.

Cluster One is composed of furs. It is a well-defined and obvious group, so further discussion of the physical aspects of this cluster should not be necessary. The presence of this well-defined cluster re-affirms the hypothesis that furs are a basic prestige-good in prestige-good systems.

In terms of social variables, the furs that compose Cluster One had no restrictions on their use or possession. They were often exchanged, usually for something other than furs, and generally for an indeterminate cost. These furs had no usual location in daily use, but were often placed in graves.

Cluster Two is a heterogeneous group of goods, mainly complex in shape and dark in color. These goods are evenly divided between plant and animal in terms of manufacturing material, although the material is generally of local origin. This cluster is composed of a mix of ornaments, utensils, and other goods. Many of these goods may be antique. They are generally rectanguloid in shape, and, as stated above, dark in color. About half have some decoration. The goods in Cluster Two come in a wide range of sizes, and have smooth surface characteristics. Acquisition labor is moderate to high, as is manufacturing labor, but durability is only moderate. Appearance is ordinary to extraordinary.

There is a tendency for the goods in Cluster Two to be restricted to adult, high-status males. Despite restrictions, the goods are often exchanged, generally for a different kind of good of equal or indeterminate value. Exchange is generally local. These goods are most often found in dwellings, and they are usually placed in graves. This description suggests that Cluster Two contains small, dark status symbols, that are generally personal ornaments or utensils.

Cluster Three is the largest of the seven clusters. It contains a variety of personal ornaments, many made from precious materials. These goods are manufactured from animal materials or precious metals that are often locally available. They are in almost all cases personal ornaments, and many of them may be antique. They are generally ovoid in form, and white

Table 4.5. Prestige-Goods in Each of Seven Clusters Defined Through the Second Cluster Analysis.

Cluster One	Cluster Three	Cluster Five
0032-sea otter fur	0001-king's crown	0018-leopard-skin tunic
0038-tanned skins	0002-gold ear-rings	0022-triple brass phallus
0048-furs	0003-gold armlet	0061-plains-type clothes
0052-furs	0004-gold ring	0091-human scalp
0060-furs	0005-gold neck chain	0094-moccasins
0065-leopard skin	0007-silver staff	0095-puberty clothes
0097-buckskin	0010-king's gold shield	0099-turquoise
0111-deerskin	0013-gold bracelet	0130-embroidered clothes
0115-deerskin	0015-silver neck chain	**Cluster Six**
0128-otter skin	0021-silver neck chain	0042-red ochre
0129-buffalo skin	0023-white turban	0078-salt
Cluster Two	0030-bone bracelet	0118-greenstone
0011-king's parasol	0039-pack-line bone	0121-whale's teeth
0025-hair comb	0040-dentalium shells	**Cluster Seven**
0026-tortoise-shell pin	0041-labrets (bone)	0006-king's cloak
0027-pandanus mats	0047-shell beads	0017-red tunic
0034-copper shield	0055-armshells	0024-feather frontlet
0037-slit gong	0056-shell necklace	0098-abalone shell
0044-dark shell money	0057-dentalium shells	0100-feathers
0096-hide shield	0075-shells	0110-woodpecker scalps
0106-pandanus mats	0076-small shell beads	0131-deer-tail headdress
0107-tapa (barkcloth)	0077-ostrich-eggshell beads	
0108-black shell money	0079-shell beads	
0112-obsidian blades	0081-labrets (bone)	
0124-crow feathers	0084-shell money	
0127-tobacco pouch	0088-embroidered headband	
Cluster Four	0101-silver necklace	
0028-tapa (barkcloth)	0105-quartz-cylinder pendant	
0029-whale's teeth	0109-white shell money	
0035-white shell money	0113-shell discs	
0036-red shell money	0114-magnesite-cylinder beads	
0043-white shell money	0116-red shell money	
0050-dentalium shells	0117-white shell money	
0083-red wood cane	0119-white heron feathers	
0087-red cloth	0120-shark's teeth	
	0122-greenstone pendant	
	0123-eagle feathers	
	0125-eagle war bonnet	

(or yellow) in color. They have little decoration, and have smooth or polished surfaces. They are all small or medium in size, and require high labor inputs for both acquisition and manufacturing, and they are also highly durable. Overall, they have a generally extraordinary appearance.

The goods in Cluster Three have a tendency to be restricted to high-status adult males. Many of the goods are symbols of political office. The goods are often exchanged for a variety of items, generally of equal value. Many of these exchanges take place between social levels, and between individuals in different communities. The goods in Cluster Three can generally be regarded as political or status symbols. These goods are sometimes placed in graves. This large cluster seems to give more support to the hypothesis that personal ornament status symbols made of precious materials are a basic category of prestige-good in prestige-good systems. This cluster, however, also contains many bead goods, and may suggest that the two hypothesized categories of status goods and bead goods should be collapsed into one.

Cluster Four is another heterogeneous group of goods, but contains a core group of shell bead goods. These goods are composed of animal material of generally non-local origin. They are generally ovoid in shape and white in color, with no additional decoration. They have a smooth surface and are small or medium in size. Acquisition and manufacturing labor are high for these goods, while durability is moderate to high. The goods have an ordinary appearance.

Socially, the goods in Cluster Four have no restrictions on them. They are frequently exchanged for various other goods of equal or indeterminate value. They are sometimes placed in graves. This cluster's description fits that of shell bead goods, and indeed a core of these goods is present. The existence of this cluster suggests that shell bead goods may indeed stand as an independent category of prestige-good, and may not have to be collapsed into a more general category of personal ornament status goods. Items in this cluster are generally not status-goods, and this gives further impetus for retaining a separate category for "shell money" or the like.

Cluster Five is a group of clothes and clothing-like personal ornaments. These goods are made of animal materials of generally local origin. They are primarily brown or tan in color, but have some secondary coloration as well. They are generally decorated, using a variety of techniques, but the designs are usually geometric. Acquisition and manufacturing labor is high, but durability for these goods is only moderate. Their appearance is often extraordinary.

The goods in Cluster Five have a slight tendency to be restricted to high-status males. These goods are sometimes exchanged, generally for other goods of indeterminate value. Exchanges sometimes take place between social levels, but usually locally. The goods in Cluster Five are status or ritual symbols that are sometimes placed in graves. Again, this cluster is a group of status symbols, but are generally more complex and larger than those of Cluster Three. They primarily have more decoration and a more complex gross form. However, they probably fit with a category of personal ornament status goods.

Cluster Six is a very small cluster of only four items. They are all valuable raw materials with few social restrictions. They are often exchanged for other goods of equal value, and are sometimes placed in graves. This cluster, although obvious and tight, is somewhat of an outlier, and does not fit well with any of the hypothesized categories of prestige-good.

Finally, Cluster Seven consists of colorful personal ornaments, manufactured from either plant or animal materials, sometimes of non-local origin. They have complex gross forms, and are often red in color, although they have a wide variety of secondary colors. The goods in Cluster Seven sometimes have additional decoration. They have smooth or composite surfaces, and are generally small. Acquisition labor is high, but manufacturing labor and durability vary. Their appearance is generally extraordinary.

The goods in Cluster Seven have a tendency to be restricted to high-status male political office holders. They are exchanged, but not frequently. These goods tend to be symbols of ritual or political office, and are sometimes placed in graves. Once again, these goods seem to fit with the hypothesized category of personal ornament status-goods.

Conclusions from the Cluster Analyses

The cluster analyses support the existence of three of the four hypothesized categories of prestige-goods, and suggest the potential for an additional category. Furs seem to be an obvious category of prestige-goods, as hypothesized (and represented by Cluster 1). Bead goods, particularly shell beads, also seem to form a category, also as hypothesized (and partly represented by Cluster 4). The hypothesized category of status goods appears to be further divided. One apparent category of status good seems to be small personal ornaments of precious, durable materials with little additional decoration (represented by Cluster 3). A second apparent category of status good seems to be larger and more complex personal ornaments, often of natural materials and less durable, but with more decoration and color than the first category (represented by Clusters 2,5, and 7). This category also tends to be associated with ritual and political offices. The hypothesized category of cloth goods did not appear in any of the analyses.

The analyses suggest four categories of prestige-good: (1) furs; (2) bead goods (particularly shell beads); (3) small personal ornaments of durable precious materials; and (4) larger, more complex personal ornaments of less durable, often natural materials. The first category seems to be one of simple, valuable items. The second of more standardized, money-like items. The third consists of status symbols, and the fourth of political or ritual office symbols. I must admit, however, that the distinction between status symbols and political or ritual symbols is not statistically significant, at least for this data set.

There are some obvious problems with these categories, and with the cluster analyses in general. Perhaps one of the most obvious problems is that the categories, and the analyses, are highly interpretive. But this is the nature of cluster analysis. Cluster analysis is not a rigorous or highly formal technique. It is a technique that brings out patterns in a data set, but what those patterns mean are left up to the interpreter. As Michael Anderberg (1973:176) explains:

> The use of cluster analysis requires the active participation of the analyst to interpret the results and judge their significance. This stage of the process is subjective, intuitive, and heuristic...A large part of this interpretive stage is a matter of the analyst using his powers of judgment and subjective evaluation to find regularities and relations "by inspection."

It is because interpreting the results of a cluster analysis is highly subjective that I have attempted to offer the reader as much information about the analyses performed as possible, and to include as much raw data as possible.

Another obvious problem is that the clusters are not as tight as might be desired or expected. The simple fact is that there was tremendous variation in the data. There is a wide variety of goods that are used in prestige-good systems, and the prestige-good systems considered for these analyses were extremely diverse themselves. A glance at Table 4.4 shows this diversity plainly, and Table 4.6, a correlation matrix for the variables used in the cluster analyses, shows the diversity more formally. Correlations, in general, were not high, and without high correlations, cluster analysis will not form tight groups. Indeed, I find it exciting that several very tight groups were identifiable given the weak correlations present in the data. Any understandable or patterned clustering is meaningful, I believe, given these weak correlations.

The Social Aspects of Prestige-Goods

It is interesting to notice how well the social variables correlated with the physical variables for these objects. Recall that only the physical variables were used for clustering. The fact that the social variables correlated well with clusters determined from the physical variables suggests that there are different types of goods serving distinct functions within these prestige-good systems. This fact might help one understand the role various types of goods play in other prestige-good systems, and I will consider this

in more detail in a moment. In general it seems that the more complex and colorful the object, the more likely it is to be a political or ritual office symbol. The simpler the object, the more likely it is to be a status symbol. And the more natural the object, the more likely it is to be simply an item of value for exchange.

Indeed this apparent correlation between an object's physical characteristics and its social characteristics is statistically significant. Table 4.7 shows the results of a t-test comparing the less ornate clusters of goods (1, 4, 6) with the more ornate clusters (2, 3, 5, 7) in terms of a computed variable called SOCIAL. I created SOCIAL as a measure of the amount of social meaning an object carried. Social meaning, in this context, refers to the amount of information an object conveys about the social, political, or ritual situation of the bearer. I recoded the variables SOCRES and CHAR, as shown in Table 4.7, so that there would be a general increase in an object's coded score as the social meaning of the object increased (as was already the case with RITRES), and computed SOCIAL by simply summing the scores on SOCRES, RITRES, and CHAR, using only those cases with a value of 5 or less for these variables (making "combination" and "other" missing values). A score of 3 on SOCIAL, then, meant that an object had little social meaning, while a score of 15 meant it carried great social meaning.

The result of the t-test is obviously significant. There is a strong difference between these clusters in terms of the social meanings they carry. This significant difference holds up when comparing the two groups on each of the separate variables used to compute SOCIAL, and the general pattern holds true when comparing each cluster with every other cluster. It appears that more ornate goods carry more social meaning than less ornate goods in prestige-good systems.

Prestige-Goods and Political Centralization

I feel compelled to ask why the physical characteristics of these prestige-goods correlate so well with their social characteristics. The social characteristics are certainly not inherent in the goods. The answer lies, I think, in the fact that the more ornate goods are favored in politically complex prestige-good systems.

More politically complex systems will contain more social, political, and ritual structures (see Blanton et al. 1981:21-22). This complexity creates more information to be conveyed about social, political, and ritual status. Any prestige-good employed has the potential to convey more information than if it were being used in a less complex system. If more politically complex systems do indeed favor more ornate goods, then one should expect these goods to convey more social meaning, simply because there is more information to convey in these systems. Social meaning, in this sense,

Table 4.6. Correlation matrix for variables used in the cluster analysis.

	PMT	PMO	CLASS	FORM	PC	ACQ	MAN	DUR	APP
PMT	1.0000 (127) P= .	.1777 (116) P= .028	-.0442 (127) P= .311	-.0398 (125) P= .330	-.1101 (102) P= .135	.3154 (123) P= .000	.0964 (121) P= .147	.3716 (124) P= .000	.1780 (124) P= .024
PMO	.1777 (116) P= .028	1.0000 (116) P= .	.0188 (116) P= .420	-.1578 (114) P= .047	-.2996 (96) P= .002	.4108 (112) P= .000	.0779 (110) P= .209	.1847 (113) P= .025	-.1412 (113) P= .068
CLASS	-.0442 (127) P= .311	.0188 (116) P= .420	1.0000 (132) P= .	.4278 (127) P= .000	.3739 (102) P= .000	-.0602 (123) P= .254	-.3038 (121) P= .000	-.1869 (124) P= .019	-.3632 (124) P= .000
FORM	-.0398 (125) P= .330	-.1578 (114) P= .047	.4278 (127) P= .000	1.0000 (127) P= .	.4432 (101) P= .000	.0531 (121) P= .281	-.4737 (120) P= .000	-.3895 (122) P= .000	-.2996 (122) P= .000
PC	-.1101 (102) P= .135	-.2996 (96) P= .002	.3739 (102) P= .000	.4432 (101) P= .000	1.0000 (102) P= .	-.2203 (99) P= .014	-.0788 (98) P= .220	-.1810 (100) P= .036	-.1511 (100) P= .067
ACQ	.3154 (123) P= .000	.4108 (112) P= .000	-.0602 (123) P= .254	.0531 (121) P= .281	-.2203 (99) P= .014	1.0000 (123) P= .	.0402 (120) P= .331	.2697 (123) P= .001	.1452 (122) P= .055
MAN	.0964 (121) P= .147	.0779 (110) P= .209	-.3038 (121) P= .000	-.4737 (120) P= .000	-.0788 (98) P= .220	.0402 (120) P= .331	1.0000 (121) P= .	.3726 (121) P= .000	.6019 (121) P= .000
DUR	.3716 (124) P= .000	.1847 (113) P= .025	-.1869 (124) P= .019	-.3895 (122) P= .000	-.1810 (100) P= .036	.2697 (123) P= .001	.3726 (121) P= .000	1.0000 (124) P= .	.2422 (123) P= .003
APP	.1780 (124) P= .024	-.1412 (113) P= .068	-.3632 (124) P= .000	-.2996 (122) P= .000	-.1511 (100) P= .067	.1452 (122) P= .055	.6019 (121) P= .000	.2422 (123) P= .003	1.0000 (124) P= .

(COEFFICIENT / (CASES) / 1-TAILED SIG)

Table 4.7. T-Test Comparing Social Meanings of Goods in Clusters 1,4, and 6 With Those of Clusters 2, 3, 5, and 7.

Recoded SOCRES (Social restrictions on object):

1-none	4-high status
2-lowest status	5-highest status
3-low status	9-unknown

Recoded CHAR (Social characteristics of object):

1-none	4-ritual symbol
2-age symbol	5-political symbol
3-status symbol	9-unknown

SOCIAL = RITRES + SOCRES + CHAR

T-Test Results:
Group 1 - Clusters 1,4,6
Group 2 - Clusters 2,3,5,7

Variable=SOCIAL

	N	Mean	S.D.	S.E.
Group 1	18	3.777	0.957	0.181
Group 2	52	7.961	0.589	0.636

T-value	D.F.	Probability
-5.32	64.91	.000 (separate variance estimate)

is epiphenomenal to the selection of particular goods by systems of differing political complexity.

To test this hypothesis, I divided the sample of 27 prestige-good systems described earlier into two groups, Group One consisting of 17 less politically centralized societies, and Group Two consisting of 10 more politically centralized societies. I based this division upon the society's score on seven variables from the *World Cultures* database. I used variables 76 (Community Leadership), 77 (Local Political Succession), 83 (Levels of Sovereignty), 85 (Executive), 89 (Judiciary), 90 (Police), and 91 (Administrative Hierarchy) to measure the political centralization of the 27 sample prestige-good systems. Table 4.8 shows the coded values for these variables, and Table 4.9 shows how each society scored. If a society's summed score on these seven variables was greater than the average for the 27 societies (18.5), then I considered it to have greater political centralization than a society that had a summed score less than the average.

Table 4.10 presents a crosstabulation of political centralization with the four categories of prestige-goods described through the previous analyses. For the purpose of this crosstabulation, I combined

Cluster One and Cluster Six to represent the category of furs (and raw materials). I used Cluster Four to represent the category of shell or bead goods, and Cluster Three to represent the category of small personal ornaments. I combined Clusters Two, Five, and Seven to represent the category of ornate personal ornaments. I performed a chi-square test on this crosstabulation using the CROSSTABS program in SPSSX (SPSS, Inc. 1988) in order to determine if the clusters used by the two groups differed significantly, and the chi-square statistic supports the hypothesis that there is a significant difference between the categories of prestige-goods used by less politically centralized prestige-good systems and those used by more politically centralized prestige-good systems.

It appears from Table 4.10 that less politically centralized prestige-good systems are more likely to employ categories of prestige-goods that are furs, and less likely to employ categories of goods that are ornate personal ornaments. On the other hand, prestige-good systems that are more politically centralized are more likely to use categories of prestige-goods that are ornate personal ornaments, and less likely to use categories that are furs. This strongly supports the

Table 4.8. Variables Used to Determine Degree of Political Centralization.

Variable 76 - Community Leadership
1 = no centralized local leadership
2 = higher level only
3 = single local leader
4 = dual/plural headman
5 = single local leader and council
6 = local councils
7 = single local leader and subordinates
8 = too complex to be coded

Variable 77 - Local Political Succession
1 = no headman or council
2 = by appointment
3 = seniority
4 = divination
5 = informal concensus
6 = electoral process
7 = patrilineal
8 = matrilineal
9 = hereditary with personal qualifications

Variable 83 - Levels of Sovereignty
1 = stateless society
2 = sovereignty 1st hierarchical level
3 = sovereignty 2nd hierarchical level
4 = sovereignty 3rd or higher hierarchical level

Variable 85 - Executive
1 = absent
2 = council
3 = executive and council
4 = plural executive
5 = single leader

Variable 89 - Judiciary
1 = absent
2 = not local
3 = executive
4 = appointed by executive
5 = priesthood
6 = hereditary

Variable 90 - Police
1 = not specialized
2 = incipient specialization
3 = retainers of chiefs
4 = military
5 = specialized

Variable 91 - Administrative Hierarchy
1 = absent
2 = popular assemblies
3 = heads of kin groups
4 = heads of decentralized territorial divisions
5 = heads of centralized territorial divisions
6 = part of a centralized system

Table 4.9. Scores for Each Society on Measures of Political Centralization. Variables as Columns.

76	77	83	85	89	90	91	Society Number	Total
7	7	3	3	3	1	6	0004	30
5	7	2	3	3	1	4	0005	25
2	1	4	5	3	.	5	0033	21
1	1	1	1	1	1	1	0090	7
5	5	1	1	1	1	1	0097	15
5	8	1	1	1	1	1	0098	18
5	2	1	1	1	1	1	0099	12
8	7	4	5	3	1	4	0102	32
5	7	2	2	1	1	3	0103	21
5	7	1	1	1	1	1	0104	17
5	7	1	1	1	1	1	0105	17
7	9	2	3	3	5	2	0106	31
5	5	1	1	1	1	1	0113	15
6	3	1	1	1	1	1	0122	14
5	8	2	5	1	1	4	0130	26
3	8	1	1	1	1	1	0131	16
5	5	1	1	1	1	1	0133	15
1	1	1	1	1	1	1	0134	7
4	8	1	1	1	1	1	0135	17
3	5	1	1	1	1	1	0138	13
6	5	1	1	1	2	1	0143	17
5	8	3	2	3	1	4	0144	26
7	9	1	1	1	5	1	0145	25
5	5	2	5	1	1	4	0148	23
3	5	1	1	1	1	1	0157	13
3	7	1	1	1	1	1	0167	15
3	5	1	1	1	1	1	0172	13

Mean = 18.5

hypothesis that more politically complex prestige-goods systems use goods that are more ornate than less politically complex prestige-good systems. In turn, this serves to answer the question posed above: more ornate prestige-goods carry more social meaning because they are used by societies that have more social information to convey through the goods.

Political Centralization and the Control of Prestige-Goods

This answer, however, only serves to create another question: why do more politically complex societies use more ornate prestige-goods? The answer to this question, I think, is that the goods I have been calling ornate can also be thought of as being more readily controllable than other categories of prestige-

goods, and more politically centralized prestige-good systems tend to employ prestige-goods that can be monopolistically controlled to a greater degree (Peregrine 1991b).

In the last chapter I argued that social evolution is related to changes in trade density. Given the nature of political power in prestige-good systems, one might expect changes in the nature of prestige-goods themselves to accompany political centralization. Political power in prestige-good systems is based upon the control of prestige-goods. As political centralization increases, and political leaders gain more power to affect the system, one should expect them to favor goods more suitable for monopoly control, perhaps changing the entire nature of the prestige-good system.

Table 4.10. Crosstabulation Comparing Categories of Goods Used in Prestige-Good Systems of Differing Political Centralization.

	furs(raw material)	shell/bead goods	small ornament	ornate ornament
Less centralized				
observed frequency	12	5	23	11
expected frequency	8.5	4.5	21.5	16.4
More centralized				
observed frequency	3	3	15	18
expected frequency	6.5	3.5	16.5	12.5

Chi-Square			
	Value	df	Sig.
Pearson	7.812	3	.05
Likelihood Ratio	8.086	3	.04

Table 4.11 shows the seven clusters of prestige-goods defined in the analyses above in terms of their potential to be monopolistically controlled. The first column shows whether the cluster contains goods that are common wealth indicators. A common wealth indicator is an item that is recognized as being valuable by members of a society, and that is obtainable by anyone with sufficient resources. If the cluster contains common wealth indicators, then its potential to be monopolistically controlled is limited, for the goods it contains are not necessarily restricted for use by a particular segment of the society. Control of these goods is based on the fact that most individuals are not wealthy enough to obtain them, but there are no direct limitations on their distribution.

The second column shows whether the cluster contains goods that are often exchanged for use value. Exchange for use value refers to a transaction in which a particular good is exchanged for another good or service of equal perceived value, with few or no restrictions on what that good or service is. In a situation where prestige-goods can be exchanged for use value, the potential for control is limited, for an individual can obtain prestige-goods by offering goods of another type or simple labor service. This means that through individual barter or labor virtually everyone can obtain prestige-goods, without having to go through a controlling "middle-man" or political office holder. It should be obvious that the potential for monopolistic control of goods that can be exchanged for use value is very low.

The third column shows whether the goods in the cluster are made of rare or exotic materials. Often these materials are of non-local origin, and their acquisition can be controlled through political personnel interacting with foreign polities. In addition, these materials frequently come from point sources, which can also be more readily controlled than dispersed sources. The simple fact that these materials are rare makes them amenable to control, for there are few to keep track of or to disseminate through a population. If a cluster contains goods made of exotic or rare materials, then, its potential to be monopolistically controlled is high.

The fourth column shows whether the goods in the cluster require specialized labor to be produced. Specialized labor is labor that cannot be done by an ordinary person. It requires special education, special skills, or an extraordinary amount of time. Recalling Meillassoux's (1978:138) discussion of the basis of political power in prestige-good systems, a major aspect was the control of esoteric knowledge. Specialized manufacturing techniques are an obvious form of esoteric knowledge, and are amenable to control in prestige-good systems. Since political leaders may be able to control access to this knowledge, and in turn, the specialized laborers who employ it, then there is again the potential for clusters containing items that require specialized labor to be monopolistically controlled (Peregrine 1991b).

The fifth column shows the overall potential for the goods in the cluster to be monopolistically controlled, based on how the goods rank in terms of the other four columns. The goods in Cluster One, for example, are common wealth indicators, and are frequently exchanged for use value. They are common materials, and require little or no specialized labor; therefore, they have little potential to be monopolistically

Table 4.11. Potential for Goods in Clusters to be Monopolistically Controlled.

Cluster	Common Wealth Indicator	Exchanged For Use Value	Rare/ Exotic Material	Specialized Labor Required	Potential For Monopolistic Control
Cluster 1	Y	Y	N	N	Low
Cluster 2	N	?	Y	Y	High
Cluster 3	N	Y	Y	Y	Moderate
Cluster 4	Y	Y	N	?	Low
Cluster 5	N	N	?	Y	High
Cluster 6	Y	Y	N	N	Low
Cluster 7	N	N	Y	Y	High

Table 4.12. Location of Clusters in Terms of Degree of Political Centralization.

Less Centralized	⟷	Semi-Centralized	⟷	More Centralized
Cluster 1				Cluster 2
Cluster 4		Cluster 3		Cluster 5
Cluster 6				Cluster 7

Table 4.13. General Correlates for the Types of Goods Used in Less Politically Centralized and More Politically Centralized Prestige-Good Systems.

Less Centralized	⟷	More Centralized
few precious metals		more precious metals
few decorated goods or goods with specialized labor		more decorated goods or goods with specialized labor
few social restrictions on possession of goods		sex restrictions (male), status restrictions, and political office restrictions on goods
goods are sometimes destroyed		goods are rarely destroyed

controlled. The goods in Cluster Seven, on the other hand, are neither common wealth indicators nor exchanged. They are often made of rare and exotic materials, and require specialized labor to be produced; therefore, they have a relatively high potential to be monopolistically controlled.

Table 4.12 shows the locations of the seven clusters in terms of their potential to be monopolistically controlled, and in terms of their hypothesized relationships with political centralization. These relationships parallel those determined through the crosstabulation of the clusters with political centralization, as described above. Table 4.12 strongly supports the hypothesis that more politically centralized prestige-good systems employ categories of goods that are more amenable to monopolistic control

than less politically centralized prestige-good systems.

Prestige-Goods Used in Systems of Differing Political Centralization

In order to more fully explore the differences in the types of prestige-goods used in systems of differing political centralization, I compared the coded values for prestige-goods used by less centralized and more centralized systems in the sample across all the variables using the CROSSTABS program in SPSSX (SPSS, Inc. 1988). Table 4.13 offers a summary of significant differences (I used the 0.1 level of significance because of the small sample size and the data problems discussed earlier) in the nature of prestige-goods used by less politically centralized and more politically centralized systems. It appears that more politically centralized prestige-good systems tend to use more ornate goods, goods requiring specialized labor, and goods made of rare or exotic materials. Goods in more politically centralized systems also tend to carry more restrictions, so that their distribution within the society deviates markedly from random. From this information I developed a number of testable hypotheses that allow assessment of the Mississippian prestige-good system. I develop and test these hypotheses in the next chapter.

5

The Mississippian Prestige-Good System

In this chapter I use the information gained about prestige-goods and prestige-good systems in previous chapters to look at the material record of Mississippian societies in order to determine if they were participants in a prestige-good system. This is a difficult problem in an archaeological context, for prestige-good systems are defined in terms of social patterns and political strategies, not in terms of the material goods themselves. One cannot simply look for the presence of prestige-goods and from their presence conclude that a prestige-good system existed, for prestige-goods are not restricted to prestige-good systems—examples can be found in virtually all societies. Rather, one must look at the way in which prestige-goods are used and controlled. It is the distribution of prestige-goods within a society (or a group of interacting societies) that must be considered in order to demonstrate the presence or absence of a prestige-good system in an archaeological context.

My initial task in this chapter, therefore, is to use the knowledge gained about prestige-goods and prestige-good systems in previous chapters to develop a model and set of hypotheses about the distribution of prestige-goods in prestige-good systems. I can then use this model and its associated hypotheses to look at the material record for the Mississippian period (and the distribution of prestige-goods), in order to determine if a prestige-good system existed.

Using Table 4.13 and the discussion at the end of Chapter Two as a guide for this model, it appears that if a prestige-good system is in operation one should expect that populations located in communities where high-level political personnel are resident will have access to more prestige-goods than populations in communities lacking resident high-level political personnel, and particularly more exotic or ornate goods. Most prestige-goods will be in the hands of high-level political office holders, generally adult males, so one should expect the distribution of goods within communities to be skewed towards adult males. Since these political personnel are actively controlling access to prestige-goods, one should expect that their distribution within and between communities will be skewed as well. This simple model suggests at least three hypotheses.

Hypothesis One

The first hypothesis one can derive from the model is that there should be more prestige-goods where high-level political personnel are resident than in other communities, and particularly more exotic or ornate goods. Again, this makes sense given the nature of political strategy in prestige-good systems. Power in prestige-good systems is based upon the control of prestige-goods, so those in power should possess more of them. As discussed in the last chapter, high-level political personnel should actively favor goods amenable to control—goods that are made of exotic or rare materials, and goods requiring specialized labor to be produced. So, one should expect there to be not only more prestige-goods where political leaders are located, but particularly more exotic or ornate prestige-goods.

Hypothesis Two

A second hypothesis one can derive from the model is that prestige-goods should be found more often in the hands of adult males. The reason for this follows from the discussion above. Political office holders control prestige-goods, and thereby possess more of them. Political office holders, in turn, are generally both male and adult.

I examined six prestige-good systems in Chapters 2 and 3. In all cases the main political personnel (and the major possessors of prestige-goods) were adult males. Indeed, this makes complete sense if one recalls Meillassoux's discussion of basic political strategies in prestige-good systems. According to Meillassoux (1978:139), the control of prestige-goods and esoteric knowledge is a means by which adult males control juveniles' access to social positions and, ultimately, to nubile women within a lineage. Earlier in this study I argued that prestige-good systems evolve in the framework of a lineage structure, with adult males serving as lineage elders becoming the political leaders in prestige-good systems that evolve through them. One must conclude that adult males are the major political figures in prestige-good systems, and hence the major controllers of prestige-goods. The distribution of prestige-goods will therefore be skewed towards adult males.

Again, one can also expect that adult males, as political office holders, will actively favor goods amenable to control. The distribution of prestige-good types should therefore also be skewed, with adult males possessing more exotic or ornate goods.

Hypothesis Three

A third hypothesis one can derive from the model is that the distribution of prestige-goods flowing out of political centers should form a distribution that suggests restricted exchange. In other words, political leaders should not be allowing goods to be freely exchanged within the system, but should be directing goods to particular individuals or communities. Political power in prestige-good systems is based upon the control of prestige-goods. Political leaders must actively restrict access to goods, and constrain their distribution. Prestige-goods are allowed to be possessed only by chosen individuals or groups, not by all members of the society. For this reason, the distribution of goods between communities in the system should be highly constrained if a prestige-good system exists. A distribution suggesting unrestricted exchange would violate the fundamental process of such systems: the control of prestige-goods.

Testing for the Mississippian Prestige-Good System

Testing these hypotheses requires a standard unit of comparison so that I can measure the distribution of prestige-goods within and between communities.

The simplest way to do this is to consider the numbers and types of goods being used per capita. For archaeologically-known societies, I can easily determine the number and types of prestige-goods in use per capita with information from excavated burials. Recall from the previous chapter that prestige-goods are usually buried with their possessor, so it is reasonable to assume that if an individual had access to a certain type and quantity of prestige-good, that this would be reflected in the goods buried with them.

Indeed, many other researchers have confirmed a connection between an individual's social position in life and their burial accompaniments (for examples see Brown 1971; Chapman, Kinnes, and Randsborg 1981; Tainter 1978; dissenting views can be found in Hodder 1982 and Parker Pearson 1982). It also makes sense that in prestige-good systems political leaders would want goods buried with their possessor. This would take the goods out of circulation, and allow the political leader to maintain control over the deceased's descendants, who might otherwise have acquired their ancestor's prestige-goods. By studying burial populations, then, I can readily examine the distribution of prestige-goods.

Revised Hypotheses

With this standard unit to measure the distribution of prestige-goods in Mississippian communities (number of goods per excavated burial), I can revise the three hypotheses above and create test implications for each.

Hypothesis One states that there should be more prestige-goods in locations where high-level political personnel are present than in more peripheral locations. In terms of the Mississippian period, there should be more prestige-goods on sites that were chiefdom centers, and less of these materials on outlying sites. Chiefdom centers for the Mississippian period are easily identified. According to Bruce Smith (1978:496) they can be defined in terms of (1) large overall size, (2) evidence of corporate labor expenditure in the form of mounds, fortifications, and the like, (3) the presence of high-status burials and exotic goods, and (4) a reasonable high spatial efficiency with respect to outlying communities. These centers also contain chiefly residences, ceremonial buildings, and other structures that strongly suggest highest-level political personnel were resident at them (Peebles and Kus 1977).

Using burial data, one should find that (1) the proportion of excavated burials from Mississippian chiefdom centers that contain prestige-goods should be higher than the proportion for peripheral areas, and (2) the average number of these goods per burial should be higher for Mississippian chiefdom centers than for peripheries. I will measure both proportion and average as it has been suggested that data on burial goods frequently form distributions more similar to Poisson (binary) than to Gaussian (normal)(see Hatch 1974:100).

In addition, Hypothesis One suggests that there may be more exotic or rare goods where high-level political personnel are resident than in more peripheral areas. So, one can also expect excavated burials from Mississippian chiefdom centers to contain both (1) a higher proportion and (2) a higher average number of these goods than peripheral burials.

Hypothesis Two states that the distribution of prestige-goods should be skewed towards adult males. Considering this in terms of Mississippian burials, one should find that (1) the proportion of adult male burials containing prestige-goods should be higher than the proportion of either females or juvenile males, and (2) the number of prestige-goods per adult male burial should be higher, on average, than either females or juvenile males.

Once again, Hypothesis Two suggests that an effect might also be present in terms of the types of prestige-goods possessed by adult males. One can expect that the distribution of exotic or ornate goods, both (1) proportionally and (2) on average, will also be skewed towards adult males.

Hypothesis Three states that the distribution of prestige-goods flowing out of political centers should form a highly constrained distribution. If goods were leaving Mississippian centers without restrictions, that is, if political leaders were distributing goods freely to individuals in peripheral communities rather than directing them to particular individuals in particular communities, the distribution of their final locations, in terms of their distance from center plotted against the number of goods found at that distance, would be Gaussian (see Berg 1983, also Renfrew 1977:85-86, 1975:48-51, 1972:470-71; Fry 1979:497). The distribution of prestige-goods between Mississippian communities, then, should be distinctly non-Gaussian and should show a constrained distribution.

Goods received from political leaders should not be freely exchanged either. Once again, political power in prestige-good systems is a product of an individual's control over prestige-goods. Goods, therefore, should produce a distribution reflecting this control, and not one reflecting free exchange. If individuals were simply exchanging goods down-the-line, taking a portion of goods received from a center and passing the rest on, the resulting distribution (distance from center plotted against number of goods) would be exponential (Renfrew 1977:77-79, 1975:46-48; Fry 1979:497). Mississippian

prestige-goods, then, should not show an exponential distribution either.

The only type of regular distribution that may, in some circumstances, be expected in a prestige-good system is linear. A linear distribution would suggest that the amount of prestige-goods reaching a community is directly proportional to its distance from center. In some cases, this might occur in a prestige-good system. Leaders at political centers must distribute prestige-goods, but they need to maintain both a stockpile of goods and control over the goods they distribute. A balance must be met between the need to distribute, the desire to possess, and the need to restrict access to goods. One strategy for striking this balance might be to distribute most goods to immediate locals, the day-to-day supporters, less to more peripheral individuals, and even less to those on the edges of the leader's sphere of influence (assuming impermeable borders to the system). The resulting distribution in this situation may approximate a linear one.

Of course, many situations might arise to distort a linear trend: if the system's boundaries are relatively permeable, individuals at the boundaries might be supplied with more goods in order to keep them loyal and part of the system; individuals producing commodities necessary to the center but distant from it might be supplied with more goods to stimulate their production; a hierarchy might exist within the political structure of the system so that distant individuals are supplied with large amounts of goods to distribute locally. In short, one cannot say what the distribution of prestige-goods between Mississippian communities should be, only what it should not be: Gaussian or exponential.

Mississippian Prestige-Goods

Before I can study the distribution of Mississippian prestige-goods, however, I first have to define what they are. In the last chapter I defined four categories of prestige-goods: (1) furs, (2) bead goods, (3) small personal ornaments, and (4) complex personal ornaments. The first category, furs, has little chance of preservation in Mississippian contexts. These goods would have decayed long before archaeologists could have excavated and recorded them. Although bones left in furs after tanning or similar suggestive evidence may survive, it would be difficult, on the basis of that evidence alone, to conclude that furs were present in a burial context. The same is likely true for the fourth category, complex personal ornaments. Recall that these goods were often fashioned from natural materials, such as feathers, skins, or wood products, and these would not have survived in an archaeological context very long either. Again, although some clues to the presence of these goods might survive, the goods themselves would not, and it would be difficult to determine exactly what did once exist in a burial context.

Bead goods and small personal ornaments of durable materials, however, should have survived, and are indeed well represented in Mississippian contexts. A wide variety of bead goods are common on Mississippian sites, particularly shell beads. Indeed it was Steponaitis's (1986) suggestion that Mississippian political leaders controlled the production of shell beads which began this discussion of political power based on the control of prestige-goods in the first place. Various types of small personal ornaments, many of them manufactured from exotic materials such as copper, quartzite, and marine shell, are commonly found in Mississippian contexts as well (see Brose, Brown and Penney 1985; also Goad 1978 and Goodman 1984 for discussions of copper goods; Hatch 1974:133 for an interesting discussion of marine shell goods).

With the revised hypotheses, and the nature of Mississippian prestige-goods defined, I can now turn my attention to the material record for the Mississippian period, and determine if the burial data support the idea that a prestige-good system was in operation.

Cahokia and the American Bottom

In a recent article George Milner (1984) compared Mississippian burial populations from 26 sites in the American Bottom, and his conclusions strongly support these three hypotheses. Milner divided the burial areas into three groups: (1) outlying cemeteries; (2) non-elite cemeteries in regional centers; and (3) elite cemeteries in regional centers. He then compared these three burial areas in terms of their physical structure and the composition of the population represented in each.

Grave goods in outlying cemeteries were dominated by ceramic vessels and utilitarian goods such as chert projectile points, sandstone abraders, and shell or bone spoons and pins (Milner 1984:474). These goods fall outside the four categories of prestige-good defined in the last chapter, so it appears that non-prestige-good items dominated outlying burial assemblages, as is predicted by Hypothesis One. However, some apparent prestige-goods were found in these cemeteries, particularly copper and shell ornaments:

> Copper artifacts tended to be personal ornaments: they included such items as copper-covered pins and earspools. Marine

shell artifacts occurred more often than copper artifacts. Usually shell had been fashioned into beads, less often into gorgets or pendants. Most individuals were buried with only a few, if any, marine shell beads (Milner 1984:475).

There appeared to be few exotic or ornate goods present on peripheral sites—more common were simple shell goods. This again supports Hypothesis One.

A quite different situation is suggested by Milner's discussion of burial populations in regional centers. The major center for the American Bottom was Cahokia, and although burial data for the site is scant, Milner (1984:480) offers this summary of the elite burial areas: "Large numbers of mortuary-related artifacts, many of which were sizable, finely crafted, and fashioned from exotic materials, were often associated with elite burial areas." This statement offers additional support for Hypothesis One. There appears to be many more prestige-goods, particularly exotic or ornate ones, at Cahokia than at peripheral sites in the American Bottom.

Milner (1984:482) also offers some support for Hypothesis Two. He tells us that at Cahokia "access to these [elite] mortuary areas was, for the most part, restricted to adults," and the associated prestige-goods were also restricted. In contrast, Milner (1984:476) tells us that "Males and females of all ages were buried in the peripherally located cemeteries," and males and females were equally represented in terms of burial goods.

Data for non-elite cemeteries at Cahokia and nearby centers are not discussed at length because the available data did not allow Milner to make firm conclusions about burial goods (Milner 1984:477-79).

It appears from Milner's study that the distribution of prestige-goods in Mississippian communities supports the idea that a prestige-good system was in operation. But Milner was more interested in gross features of the burials, such as their orientation and location within communities, than with grave goods themselves, making the support he offers for Hypotheses One and Two weak. He does not offer information that would allow one to assess Hypothesis Three either. Although his study seems to support Hypotheses One and Two, and therefore the idea of a Mississippian prestige-good system, the argument is not conclusive.

Further Analysis of American Bottom Data

In order to make a more focused analysis of the distribution of prestige-goods in Mississippian communities of the American Bottom, I compared the data on grave goods from several intensively studied Mississippian cemeteries in the region. These cemeteries were the Yokem (Perino 1971a), Schild (Perino 1971b; Goldstein 1980), East St. Louis Stone Quarry (Milner 1983), and DeFrenne (Thomas 1985). Cahokia itself is not included, for despite the hundreds (and perhaps thousands) of burials excavated at the site, I could find none that were adequately described for my purposes (George Milner [personal communication] confirmed this). I coded a total of 514 burials from the four cemeteries. The codebook is given in Appendix C, and the coded data set itself can be found in Appendix E of Peregrine (1990).

Testing Hypothesis One

Unfortunately, since data for Cahokia are lacking, I cannot formally evaluate Hypothesis One for the American Bottom. As I explained in the discussion of Milner's study, the anecdotal data that has been published about Cahokia burials (for example Fowler 1974, 1977; Moorehead 1923, 1929; H. Smith 1977) do lend support to Hypothesis One, but without better published accounts neither I nor any other scholar can say much about the true characteristics of the Cahokia burial population.

Testing Hypothesis Two

With the data from the outlying cemeteries, however, I am able to evaluate Hypothesis Two. Hypothesis Two states that prestige-goods should be skewed towards adult males, and particularly exotic or ornate goods. Table 5.1 shows how three variables were computed to assess Hypothesis Two. I created the variable BEAD as the sum of all bead goods represented in the burials. I created the variable EXOTIC as the sum of all exotic materials or highly worked goods found in the burials. I used BOTH to code for antler staffs and included it as part of EXOTIC because these staffs likely represented political office symbols. I used BUN to code for wing bones, which were likely fans, and for exotic animal head and foot bones,

which were likely parts of skins. In both cases these may have represented artifacts from the category of complex personal ornaments, and hence I included them as part of EXOTIC. Finally, I created the variable GOODS as the sum of BEAD and EXOTIC, or the sum of all prestige-goods found in the burials.

Tables 5.2, 5.3, and 5.4 present the results of t-tests comparing means for the variables BEAD, EXOTIC, and GOODS for the burial population split by AGE, SEX, and a combined variable (AGESEX) that split the group into adult males and all others. I performed these tests (and all the rest appearing in this chapter) using the T-TEST procedure in SPSSX (SPSS, Inc. 1988) with default settings, and running on the Purdue University Computing Center's IBM 3090 computer. Significance levels shown are for one-tailed tests.

A glance at these tables shows an interesting pattern. Table 5.2 suggests that bead goods are skewed towards juveniles, while Table 5.3 suggests that exotic goods are significantly skewed towards adults. Both bead goods and exotic goods are significantly skewed towards males. Finally, while bead goods show only a slight skew towards adult males, exotic goods show a significant skew.

A similar pattern is present in Tables 5.5, 5.6, and 5.7, which present the results of crosstabulating the proportion of burials containing bead goods, exotic goods, or prestige-goods in general with AGE, SEX, and the combined variable AGESEX. I performed these crosstabulations (as well as the rest presented in this chapter) with the CROSSTABS procedure in SPSSX (SPSS, Inc. 1988), using default statistics. Expected frequencies are given below observed frequencies in the tables.

Table 5.5 again suggests that bead goods are strongly skewed towards juveniles, while Table 5.6 suggests that exotic goods are significantly skewed towards adults. Table 5.7 suggests that prestige-goods in general are significantly skewed towards males. Finally, it appears that while bead goods tend not to be associated with adult male burials, exotic goods are significantly associated.

These results may seem confusing. They support the idea that exotic or ornate goods are strongly associated

Table 5.1. Variables Computed for the American Bottom Data Set.

| BEAD= |
| SSBEAD+LSBEAD+SPEN+SPER+CBEAD+BBEAD |
| EXOTIC= |
| CCOV+CWORK+MRGAL+MOCH+MROTH+STCER+BOTH+BUN |
| GOODS= |
| BEAD+EXOTIC |

Table 5.2. T-Tests of Bead Goods in American Bottom Burials.
Variable - BEAD.

Group	N	Mean	S.D.
Juveniles	204	21.34	66.80
Adults	293	12.85	94.14
T-Value	D.F	1-tail Prob.	
1.18	494.81	0.12	
Group	N	Mean	S.D.
Male	122	28.45	143.71
Female	92	1.22	7.45
T-Value	D.F.	1-tail Prob.	
2.09	121.86	0.02	
Group	N	Mean	S.D.
Adult Male	120	28.92	144.86
Other	296	15.09	56.35
T-Value	D.F.	1-tail Prob.	
1.02	133.84	0.16	

Table 5.3. T-Tests of Exotic Goods in American Bottom Burials.
Variable - EXOTIC.

Group	N	Mean	S.D.
Juveniles	204	0.04	0.24
Adults	293	0.23	1.43
T-Value	D.F.	1-tail Prob.	
-2.26	315.31	0.01	
Group	N	Mean	S.D.
Male	122	0.43	2.13
Female	92	0.14	0.64
T-Value	D.F.	1-tail Prob.	
1.44	148.74	0.08	
Group	N	Mean	S.D.
Adult Male	120	0.44	2.15
Other	296	0.07	0.41
T-Value	D.F.	1-tail Prob.	
1.88	122.52	0.03	

with adult males, as Hypothesis Two suggests, but do not support the idea that adult males control prestige-goods in general. The reason for these confusing results is simple: bead goods, strongly associated with juveniles, swamp the association of exotic goods with adult males when the variable GOODS is computed. The simple fact is that there are many more bead goods present in the sample than exotic goods, and they override any effect present from the exotic goods.

The situation that does appear to obtain is that bead goods are strongly associated with juveniles (particularly males), and exotic goods with adult males. In short, a more complex situation seems to be present in this population than was expected under Hypothesis Two. However, Hypothesis Two is still supported: prestige-goods are significantly associated with males, and exotic or ornate goods particularly associated with adult males.

The behavioral implications of this pattern fit well with the way prestige-good systems function. As prestige-good systems evolve towards greater political complexity, the favored prestige-goods tend to

Table 5.4. T-Tests of All Prestige-Goods in American Bottom Burials. Variable - GOODS.

Group	N	Mean	S.D.
Juveniles	204	21.39	66.80
Adults	293	13.09	94.17
T-Value	D.F.	1-tail Prob.	
1.15	494.82	0.12	
Group	N	Mean	S.D.
Male	122	28.89	143.72
Female	92	1.36	7.46
T-Value	D.F.	1-tail Prob.	
2.11	121.86	0.02	
Group	N	Mean	S.D.
Adult Male	120	29.37	144.87
Other	296	15.16	56.34
T-Value	D.F.	1-tail Prob.	
1.04	133.83	0.15	

Table 5.5. Crosstabulation of Bead Goods in American Bottom Burials. Variable - BEAD.

	Absent	Present
Juvenile	149	55
	172.8	31.2
Adult	272	21
	248.2	44.8

Chi-square	D.F.	Significance
36.38	1	0.00

	Absent	Present
Male	106	16
	110.6	11.4
Female	88	4
	83.4	8.6

Chi-square	D.F.	Significance
4.76	1	0.03

	Absent	Present
Adult Male	104	16
	98.4	21.6
Other	237	59
	242.6	53.4

Chi-square	D.F.	Significance
2.52	1	0.11

become those most readily controllable: exotic or ornate goods. But other prestige-goods will not simply disappear; rather, their function within the system will change. Less readily controllable goods will become less important in the system, and their distribution will change, most likely moving into segments of the society that could not previously possess them.

Testing Hypothesis Three

Hypothesis Three states that the falloff of prestige-goods from Mississippian centers should not be Gaussian or exponential, and may be linear. Again, without the data for Cahokia, I cannot make a formal assessment of Hypothesis Three. However, the falloff of goods between the peripheral sites considered here should reflect the overall falloff pattern from the center. That is, if the falloff from center to periphery was either Gaussian or exponential, a regular falloff pattern should still be present when looking only at the peripheral sites.

Figures 5.1, 5.2, and 5.3 show the number of bead goods, exotic goods, and prestige-goods in general present on these sites, plotted against their linear distance (in kilometers) from Cahokia. It is obvious that no regular pattern is present. Indeed, the large volume of prestige-goods present on the Schild site skews these plots almost beyond interpretation. In order to see if the extreme volume of prestige-goods found at the Schild site was masking a regular falloff pattern among the other sites, I repeated the plots without the Schild site, and again, there was no obvious or regular falloff pattern present. Therefore, Hypothesis Three appears to be supported.

Conclusions

Data from American Bottom peripheral cemeteries gives strong support to the idea that a prestige-good system was in operation there during the Mississippian period. All three hypotheses were supported by the available data, although better data for Cahokia could have made the support more solid.

Table 5.6. Crosstabulation of Exotic Goods in American Bottom Burials. Variable - EXOTIC.

	Absent	Present
Juvenile	198	6
	192.1	11.9
Adult	270	23
	275.9	17.1

Chi-square	D.F.	Significance
5.27	1	0.02

	Absent	Present
Male	107	15
	110	12
Female	86	6
	83	9

Chi-square	D.F.	Significance
1.98	1	0.16

	Absent	Present
Adult Male	105	15
	112.2	7.8
Other	284	12
	276.8	19.2

Chi-square	D.F.	Significance
10.04	1	0.00

Table 5.7. Crosstabulation of Prestige-Goods in American Bottom Burials. Variable - GOODS.

	Absent	Present
Juvenile	146	58
	163.8	40.2
Adult	253	40
	235.2	57.8

Chi-square	D.F.	Significance
16.59	1	0.00

	Absent	Present
Male	95	27
	100.9	21.1
Female	82	10
	76.1	15.9

Chi-square	D.F.	Significance
4.65	1	0.03

	Absent	Present
Adult Male	93	27
	92.6	27.4
Other	228	68
	228.4	67.6

Chi-square	D.F.	Significance
0.01	1	0.91

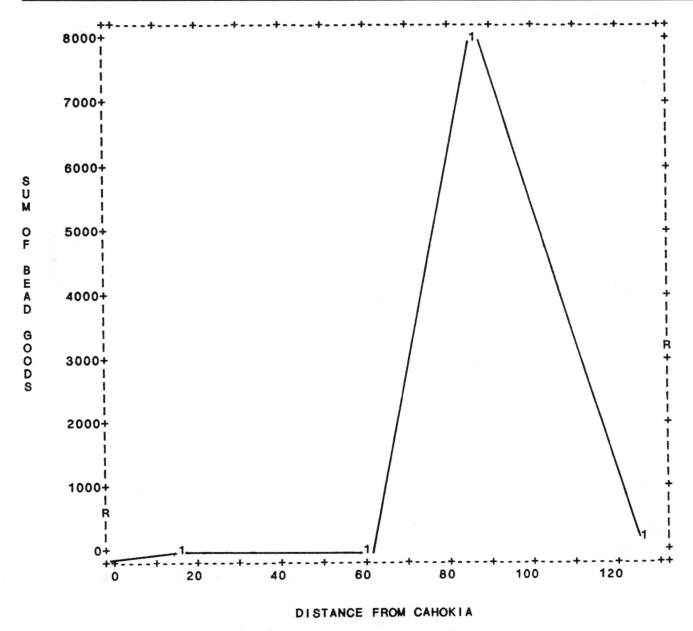

Figure 5.1. Plot of bead goods by distance from Cahokia.

In addition, the idea that a prestige-good system was in operation increases our understanding of the data. It would be difficult to interpret the distribution of goods in the American Bottom without considering these sites as participants in a prestige-good system. One would not readily understand why exotic goods are skewed towards adult males while other goods are not, and one would not understand why the distribution of these goods broke down along the lines of bead goods and exotic goods. Indeed, the fact that the distribution of goods did break down along the lines of the categories of prestige-goods established in the last chapter, and that their use in Mississippian society appears to parallel the way these categories of goods are used in other prestige-good systems, lends additional credence to the idea that a prestige-good system was in operation in the American Bottom during the Mississippian period.

The Little Tennessee and Toqua

Having looked at a group of peripheral sites without data about their center, I will now consider a central site without adequate data about its periphery. Toqua was a major Dallas focus Mississippian center on the Little Tennessee River, and was the subject of extensive

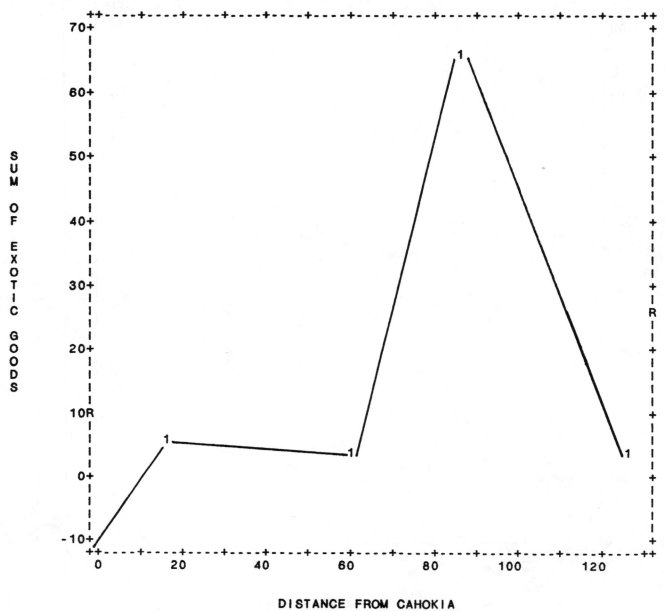

Figure 5.2. Plot of exotic goods by distance from Cahokia.

excavation by the Tennessee Valley Authority and the University of Tennessee (Chapman 1985, Polhemus 1987). I coded a total of 463 burials from Toqua and an adjacent Dallas focus Mississippian site (Martin Farm [Schroedl et.al. 1985]) for this study. The codebook is the same as that used for the American Bottom sites, and can be found in Appendix C. The coded data can be found in Appendix F of Peregrine (1990).

Testing Hypothesis One

Hypothesis One states that the distribution of prestige-goods, particularly exotic or ornate goods,

should be skewed towards political centers. Unfortunately, without additional data from peripheral sites, I cannot test Hypothesis One for the Little Tennessee region. It is interesting, however, to compare the volume of goods present on the Toqua site with that present on peripheral sites in the American Bottom. Table 5.8 shows these differences dramatically, and offers support for Hypothesis One. In all cases both the proportion and the average number of goods per burial is greater at the central site of Toqua than for the peripheral sites in the American Bottom.

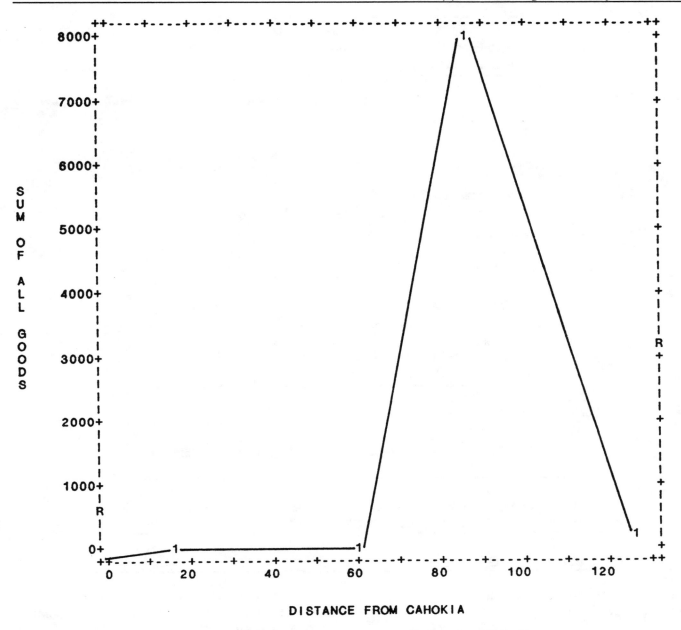

Figure 5.3. Plot of all prestige-goods by distance from Cahokia.

Testing Hypothesis Two

Table 5.9 shows how the variables BEAD, EXOTIC, and GOODS were computed for the Toqua data set. Again, I only used those goods which were represented in the burials to create these variables. I included STCER as part of EXOTIC because it was used to code for stone discoidals manufactured from exotic raw materials and showing great workmanship. SCUP represents both decorated and undecorated marine shell cups. I used SPEN to code for conch shell columns. I coded decorated pendants as SGOR.

Hypothesis Two states that prestige-goods, particularly exotic or ornate goods, should be skewed towards adult males. Tables 5.10 to 5.15 present t-tests and crosstabulations performed on the Toqua data in the same way described for the American Bottom data. The tables present a picture remarkably similar to that of the American Bottom. Table 5.13 suggests that bead goods are skewed towards juveniles. Tables 5.11 and 5.14 suggest that exotic goods are significantly skewed towards adult males. However, Tables 5.12 and 5.15 suggest that prestige-goods in general are more skewed towards adult males at Toqua than

Table 5.8. Comparison of the Proportion and Average Number of Goods Found in Burials From the American Bottom and Toqua.

Variable - BEAD	American Bottom	Toqua
Proportion	0.15	0.23
Mean	15.8	29.9
S.D.	82.6	180.2

Variable - EXOTIC	American Bottom	Toqua
Proportion	0.06	0.12
Mean	0.15	0.24
S.D.	1.09	1.02

Variable - GOODS	American Bottom	Toqua
Proportion	0.20	0.29
Mean	15.9	30.1
S.D.	82.7	180.3

Table 5.9. Variables Computed for the Little Tennessee Data Set.

BEAD=
SSBEAD+LSBEAD+SPEN+SPER+SPLUG+CBEAD+STBEAD+STPEN+ BPLUG
EXOTIC=
SGOR+SMASK+SCUP+SWORK+CPLUG+CUN+CWORK+MWMICA+MOCH+ MRGRAPH+MROTH+MQOTH+STCER
GOODS=
BEAD+EXOTIC

in the American Bottom, and offers stronger support for Hypothesis Two.

Testing Hypothesis Three

Hypothesis Three states that the falloff of goods from Mississippian centers should not be Gaussian or exponential. Without more data from peripheral sites, I cannot test Hypothesis Three for the Little Tennessee region. The one peripheral site present, Martin Farm, contained only seven Dallas focus burials, and none had grave goods. In order to evaluate Hypothesis Three, and better evaluate Hypothesis One, more data from peripheral sites is needed.

Once again, I am hindered by a lack of data. In this case, however, it is not that the data exists but is unpublished or unavailable (as is the case in the American Bottom), but that the data needed are now

under the Tellico Reservoir. Still, the information gained at Toqua offers strong support for Hypothesis Two, and some support for Hypothesis One. A pattern emerged similar to that found in the American Bottom, and this suggests that similar processes were at work in both regions. The data from Toqua suggests that it, like the American Bottom sites, was a participant in a prestige-good system.

Further Evidence

I found a very different source of evidence for the presence of a Mississippian prestige-good system in Paul Welch's 1986 dissertation (also Welch 1991). Welch analyzed the political structure of the Mississippian chiefdom at Moundville, Alabama, and concluded that the archaeological remains there seemed to fit the model of a "prestige goods

Table 5.10. T-Tests of Bead Goods in Little Tennessee Burials.
Variable - BEAD.

Group	N	Mean	S.D.
Juveniles	191	27.44	96.05
Adults	240	35.75	235.12

T-Value	D.F.	1-tail Prob.
-0.50	331.42	0.31

Group	N	Mean	S.D.
Male	110	48.45	324.37
Female	96	16.06	71.34

T-Value	D.F.	1-tail Prob.
1.02	121.19	0.15

Group	N	Mean	S.D.
Adult Male	92	56.88	354.34
Other	272	24.90	90.99

T-Value	D.F.	1-tail Prob.
0.86	95.09	0.20

Table 5.11. T-Tests of Exotic Goods in Little Tennessee Burials.
Variable - EXOTIC.

Group	N	Mean	S.D.
Juveniles	191	0.10	0.45
Adults	240	0.37	1.34

T-Value	D.F.	1-tail Prob.
-2.94	305.31	0.00

Group	N	Mean	S.D.
Male	110	0.43	1.49
Female	96	0.28	1.25

T-Value	D.F.	1-tail Prob.
0.77	203.68	0.22

Group	N	Mean	S.D.
Adult Male	92	0.49	1.61
Other	272	0.17	0.83

T-Value	D.F.	1-tail Prob.
1.83	108.01	0.03

economy." Although his "prestige goods economy" model of chiefdom structure is slightly different than that of a prestige-good system, his analyses support this chapter's premise. Welch attacked the problem of Mississippian chiefdom structure in a very different way than I am, and since he arrived at similar conclusions, his study is important to consider.

Welch's basic question concerned the political economy of the Moundville chiefdom. He began addressing this question by reviewing the controversy

Table 5.12. T-Tests of All Prestige-Goods in Little Tennessee Burials.
Variable - GOODS.

Group	N	Mean	S.D.
Juveniles	191	27.53	96.11
Adults	240	36.12	235.21

T-Value	D.F.	1-tail Prob.
-0.51	331.46	0.30

Group	N	Mean	S.D.
Male	110	48.88	324.34
Female	96	16.34	72.75

T-Value	D.F.	1-tail Prob.
1.02	121.47	0.15

Group	N	Mean	S.D.
Adult Male	92	57.37	354.29
Other	272	25.07	91.27

T-Value	D.F.	1-tail Prob.
0.86	95.11	0.19

Table 5.13. Crosstabulation of Bead Goods in Little
Tennessee Burials. Variable - BEAD.

	Absent	Present
Juvenile	139	52
	144.5	46.5
Adult	187	53
	181.5	58.5

Chi-square	D.F.	Significance
1.52	1	0.22

	Absent	Present
Male	85	25
	84.4	25.6
Female	73	23
	73.6	22.4

Chi-square	D.F.	Significance
0.04	1	0.83

	Absent	Present
Adult Male	71	21
	68	24
Other	198	74
	201	71

Chi-square	D.F.	Significance
0.68	1	0.40

Table 5.14. Crosstabulation of Exotic Goods in Little Tennessee Burials. Variable - EXOTIC.

	Absent	Present
Juvenile	179	12
	167.1	23.9
Adult	198	42
	209.9	30.1

Chi-square	D.F.	Significance
12.21	1	0.00

	Absent	Present
Male	88	22
	91.8	18.2
Female	84	12
	80.2	15.8

Chi-square	D.F.	Significance
2.09	1	0.15

	Absent	Present
Adult Male	71	21
	80.6	11.4
Other	248	24
	238.4	33.6

Chi-square	D.F.	Significance
12.44	1	0.00

Table 5.15. Crosstabulation of Prestige-Goods in Little Tennessee Burials. Variable - GOODS.

	Absent	Present
Juvenile	136	55
	133.4	57.8
Adult	165	75
	167.6	72.4

Chi-square	D.F.	Significance
0.30	1	0.58

	Absent	Present
Male	71	39
	74.8	35.2
Female	69	27
	65.2	30.8

Chi-square	D.F.	Significance
1.26	1	0.26

	Absent	Present
Adult Male	57	35
	62.7	29.3
Other	191	81
	185.3	86.7

Chi-square	D.F.	Significance
2.16	1	0.14

over Service's model of a redistributary chiefdom (Service 1971), and the current debate over whether there is a general political economy common to all chiefdoms (for example, Feinman and Neitzel 1984). Welch (1986:20-21) suggested that no one model can be said to adequately define the political economy of all chiefdoms, so in order to understand the structure of the Moundville chiefdom, one must begin by determining which model of chiefdom structure best fits the archaeological data.

Welch (1986:13-16) outlined four basic models of chiefdom political economy to compare against the material record for Moundville: (1) classic redistribution *a la* Service, (2) mobilization, where chiefs maintain stores of goods to buffer against local environmental fluctuations; (3) tributary, where tribute, particularly craft products manufactured by localized specialists, is extracted from the whole populace, but redistributed only to local elites in return for their political support; and (4) prestige goods.

Welch (1986:16) defined a prestige goods economy as one in which political leaders use tribute extracted from the whole populace as an economic base to subsidize foreign trade in prestige goods. Foreign prestige goods are redistributed to local elites, although specific items are kept by the chief and used as status symbols (Welch 1986:16). As in the tributary model, the redistributed goods never reach the whole populace, but are kept by local elites in return for their political support (Welch 1986:18).

There are three main difference between Welch's conception of a prestige goods economy and that of a prestige-good system. First, in prestige-good systems prestige-goods must be made available to local lineage leaders, and through them, to individuals—this is the very basis of power. Second, in prestige-good systems political leaders may control the production of prestige-goods that are distributed within the system rather than exclusively traded to obtain foreign goods (cf. Welch 1986:174-76)—the control of esoteric knowledge needed to produce goods is as effective a means of controlling goods as controlling their access through trade. Finally, Welch's prestige goods economy is not considered in a wider framework of inter-societal interaction, core/periphery differentiation, and competition—the things that make prestige-good systems world-systems.

These differences, however, are not extreme. Welch's conception can perhaps be seen as a simplified version of the prestige-good system model, a simplified conception based solely on Frankenstein and Rowland's (1978) article with little further research into the nature of prestige-good economies. Despite its differences, Welch's model is still very similar to the one I have developed here, and his analysis of its correlation with the material record at Moundville is therefore informative for this study.

Welch's Analysis of the Moundville Chiefdom

To test which of the four models of chiefdom structure best fit the archaeological record of the Moundville chiefdom, Welch (1986: Chapter 3) relied on excavated material from Moundville itself, from the White Site (a minor center approximately 10 kilometers from Moundville), and from material collected through surface surveys of other sites in the Moundville region. Welch, like myself, found that the data were woefully inadequate to fully evaluate the structure of this Mississippian chiefdom, but using both faunal and artifactual data he was able to come to a defendable conclusion.

Using faunal data, Welch (1986:131) found that all sites in the Moundville chiefdom had equal access to faunal resources, and could easily have been self-sufficient, suggesting that the redistribution and mobilization models do not fit the Moundville chiefdom well. However, White Site elites were apparently provisioned with deer meat (Welch 1986:100), which is consistent with both the tribute and prestige goods models.

Artifactual data suggested that some ceramics were produced by individual artisans or specialists at Moundville (Welch 1986:145-46), in addition to greenstone axes, other tools of non-local lithic material, mica ornaments, and shell beads (Welch 1986:157,163-67,171). Numerous finished artifacts of non-local origin were found both at Moundville and also at outlying sites (Welch 1986:169-70), although some non-local items, such as galena, were restricted to Moundville itself (Welch 1986:170-72).

In terms of the four models Welch began with, the Moundville chiefdom seemed to be most similar to the prestige goods economy. Classic redistribution and mobilization were not evident in the material record for Moundville because there were few differences in available resources between local communities, and no apparent specialization in production except at Moundville (Welch 1986:172). Tributary models were not well supported by the material record because outlying communities did not specialize in the production of non-utilitarian items for tribute or exchange (Welch 1986:172). The model of a prestige good economy, however, was consistent the material record for the Moundville chiefdom (Welch 1986:174,192), with one modification: the non-utilitarian goods used in foreign exchange were produced exclusively at Moundville (Welch 1986:174), and outlying communities only supported elites with subsistence goods (Welch 1986:175). While Welch (1986:176) considers this a problem in his conception of a prestige goods economy, it fits well with my model of a prestige-good system.

Conclusions

Welch's study affirms, in a very different way, the conclusions reached through the analysis of burial data from Toqua and the American Bottom—that Mississippian societies operated in the framework of a prestige-good system. Although Welch was testing a model of political economy that is slightly different from that of a prestige-good system, it is similar enough to make his conclusions valid here. The fact that his evaluation of the model's utility for understanding the political economy at Moundville was done with a very different goal than my analyses (examining which of four models best fit a specific data set as opposed to examining several sets of data to see if they fit a specific model) gives great weight to his findings. It seems clear that a prestige-good system was in operation during the Mississippian period (also see Brown et al. 1990; Peebles 1987; Steponaitis 1991).

Despite the evidence presented in this chapter, one can never say with certainty that a prestige-good system existed during the Mississippian period. Prestige-good systems are defined by a unique political strategy, which may or may not be reflected in a society's material remains. Although such a system seems to be reflected in the material remains for the Mississippian period, one can never say for certain that the system existed, for one can never see the behavior that created the pattern in the material remains. The most important question, however, is not whether a prestige-good system existed during the Mississippian period, but whether the presence of such a system informs our understanding of how Mississippian societies evolved. This question is the subject of the next chapter.

6

Evolution of the
Mississippian Prestige-Good System

The purpose of this chapter is to consider what effect the existence of a Mississippian prestige-good system would have had on the evolution of Mississippian societies. I will develop and evaluate two hypotheses to determine if I can support my contention that a prestige-good system was an active force in Mississippian evolution.

Hypothesis Four

Hypothesis Four stems from Chapter 4 where I developed and supported the idea that leaders of politically centralized prestige-good systems actively favor goods that are readily controllable (also see Peregrine 1991b). From this idea one can hypothesize that as a prestige-good system becomes more politically centralized, emergent leaders will begin to favor readily controllable prestige-goods. Because of this manipulation, the range of prestige-goods moving through the system will change as the system evolves. One can expect the goods found in communities within the system, particularly political centers, to reflect these changes.

Hypothesis Four, then, is that the range of prestige-goods present in communities within a prestige-good system will change as the system evolves towards greater political complexity. Specifically, one can expect there to be more exotic or ornate goods present in these communities as the system evolves.

Hypothesis Four can be revised for the Mississippian prestige-good system to suggest that the range of prestige-goods found in Late Woodland/Early Mississippian communities should be different from those found in Middle and Late Mississippian communities. Specifically, one should

find more exotic or ornate goods in later Mississippian occupations. I find the emergence of the "Southern Cult" during the period of greatest Mississippian fluorescence to be strong support for this hypothesis.

The "Southern Cult"

The "Southern Cult," a misnomer, as it was not necessarily a cult and was not restrained to the South (the alternate phrase, Southeastern Ceremonial Complex, doesn't help the matter much), refers to a set of artistic motifs and objects that emerged among Mississippian societies with apparent suddenness around A.D. 1250 (see Galloway 1989). Prior to this time, shell, copper, and mineral prestige-goods moved throughout the range of Mississippian societies. But with the emergence of the "Southern Cult," specific types of shell, copper, mineral, and stone prestige-goods, most with unique decorative motifs, became major elements of exchange (Waring and Holder 1945; Galloway 1989; Brown et al. 1990).

In their seminal article on the subject, "A Prehistoric Ceremonial Complex in the Southeastern United States" (1945), A.J. Waring and Preston Holder describe the various motifs and goods associated with the "Southern Cult" in detail. Decorative motifs included the cross, sun circles, bi-lobed arrow, forked eye, open eye, and various god-animal representations, among others (see Figure 6.1). Goods associated with the "Southern Cult" included such items as gorgets of marine shell or copper, conch columella pendants, embossed (repousse) copper plates, sheet-copper emblems, wood, stone, or copper ear-spools, and a variety of ceremonial celts and batons (Waring

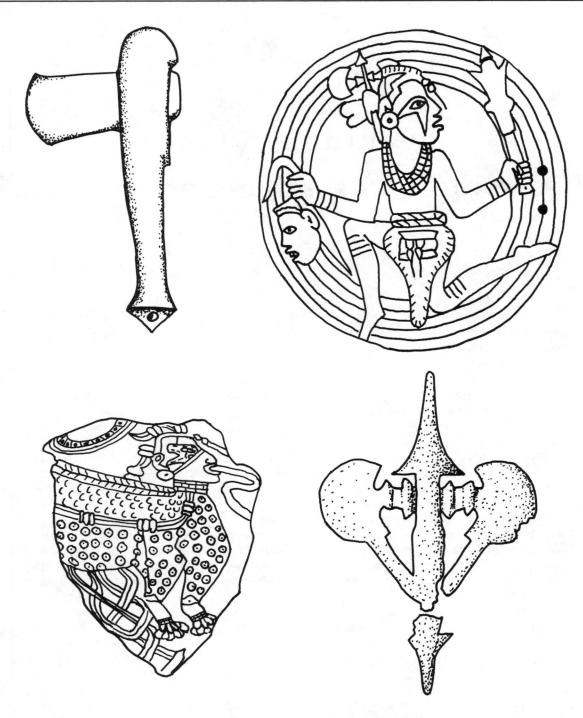

Figure 6.1. Artifacts of the Southern Cult. (Clockwise from top left: monolithic stone axe, engraved shell gorget, copper bi-lobed arrow, engraved shell cup. Adapted from Brose, Brown and Penney 1985 and Griffin 1967).

and Holder 1945:3-14). It should be obvious that these are all prestige-goods of the types described in Chapter 4 (see Brown et al. 1990 for a similar argument). And they are made particularly exotic with the addition of complex decorative motifs. Indeed, it has been argued on the basis of stylistic analyses that there may have been individual artisans responsible for large numbers of these prestige-goods (Phillips and Brown 1978).

The existence of the "Southern Cult" obviously supports Hypothesis Four. Prior to its emergence, there existed trade in prestige-goods, but the "Southern Cult" can be seen as the emergence of categories of prestige-goods more amenable to monopolistic control by political leaders in the Mississippian prestige-good system. Items of the "Southern Cult" exhibit at least three characteristics that would have made them amenable to control: (1) they were made of rare and exotic materials; (2) they required large amounts of labor to be produced; and (3) the labor for their production came from highly-skilled artisans who may have worked under the support and direction of specific political leaders.

Even without the clear example of the "Southern Cult" to lend Hypothesis Four support, data from excavated long-term Mississippian occupations give good evidence for a shift towards more readily controllable prestige-goods as Mississippian societies grew towards greater political centralization. Kenneth Orr's (1951) study of the material remains excavated at the Kincaid site in southern Illinois is a good example.

Material Culture Change at Kincaid

In his chapter "Change at Kincaid: A Study in Cultural Dynamics" (1951), Orr offers clear evidence that a shift took place in prestige-goods at the site between its major occupational components. Using data excavated from stratified mounds on the site, Orr divided the sample of non-ceramic material remains into three periods: early, middle, and late. Since the study was conducted before carbon-14 dating became common, there are no absolute dates for the material. However, the relative superpositioning of the material is sufficient for this discussion.

During the early period of occupation at Kincaid, Orr (1951:349) tells us that "bone artifacts, large points, and unworked cannel coal appear *most typical*...the Early period is characterized by a lack of...[prestige-good] types found in the Middle and Late periods." He goes on to give a more specific account of goods the early period lacks:

> The lack of effigy features in clay and stone, worked cannel coal, fluorite, galena, the finer flint artifacts,...copper, earplugs, pottery, discoidals, etc., suggests that the earlier Kincaid peoples had a less elaborate culture than that of the later people. On the other hand, the early complex did not lack the basic Middle Mississippi implements...(Orr 1951:350).

The middle period of the Mississippian occupation at Kincaid saw change in the non-ceramic material culture of the site's inhabitants. In particular, polished cannel coal disks, present in both the early and late periods, reached a height of popularity (Orr 1951:350). Many exotic goods made their first appearance during the middle period, and for that reason Orr lumps these goods with those of the late period.

The late period at Kincaid corresponds to the time when "Southern Cult" motifs and goods first made their appearance. Orr (1951:351) tells us that

> Polished picks, pestles, incised discoidals, eye-incised fragments, plaques, human statuettes, effigy rattles, pottery discoidals, human-face pipes, anvils, and copper beads occur uniquely in the Late period.

Orr (1951:351) goes on to say that many goods which first appeared in the middle period occurred in very large numbers during the late period. Among these were "copper, worked cannel coal, fluorite disk beads, worked fluorite, and galena fragments."

Orr (1951:352) summarizes his analysis of temporal change in non-ceramic goods at Kincaid in this way:

> The Early period is seen as a simpler, less highly developed stage of development than the Late period. The Late period has artifact types which...represent a greater elaboration either in form or in technique of manufacture over similar types found in the Early period.

In short, Orr tells us that the major change in non-ceramic artifacts at Kincaid from early to late periods of occupation is that form and manufacturing techniques became more complex. Again, this supports Hypothesis Four, which states that goods should become more complex or exotic as Mississippian societies evolved.

Both the emergence of the "Southern Cult" and the data from Kincaid support the idea that a shift towards prestige-goods more amenable to monopolistic control occurred as Mississippian societies became more politically centralized. The "Southern Cult" includes categories of readily controllable prestige-goods which today are used as defining markers for the period of greatest Mississippian centralization. The Kincaid site shows clear evidence of a shift towards more exotic and ornate prestige-goods (and hence, more readily controllable prestige-goods) as the site grew into a regional Mississippian center. It appears that the manipulation of prestige-goods by political leaders probably played an important role in Mississippian social evolution (also see Brown et al. 1990; Steponaitis 1991).

Hypothesis Five

Hypothesis Five stems from the basic notion that political leaders need to control prestige-goods in prestige-good systems. As a prestige-good system evolves towards greater political complexity, individuals attempting to manipulate the production and exchange of prestige-goods who are located where they can most readily control their circulation will have an advantage over less optimally-located individuals. One way in which emergent political leaders could control the circulation of prestige-goods would be to control nodal points on trade routes. One can hypothesize that emergent political leaders located at nodal points on trade routes would gain power differentially as a prestige-good system evolved, and could become the major political figures in the system because of their ability to control the circulation of prestige-goods.

Hypothesis Five, then, is that the major political personnel will emerge at nodal points on trade routes as a prestige-good system evolves towards greater political complexity. This, in turn, suggests that political centers will emerge at these same nodal locations (also see Peregrine 1991c).

Testing Hypothesis Five

Hypothesis Five suggests that political centers (settlements with resident high-level political personnel) should have developed at locations where trade in prestige-goods could be most readily controlled. For the northern range of Mississippian societies, trade in prestige-goods was almost certainly conducted along the river systems. Robert Lafferty (1977) offers a lucid defense of this proposition in Appendix I of his dissertation. Lafferty (1977:53,171) argues that riverine travel would have been more than twice as efficient as overland travel, and offers strong documentary evidence that riverine travel was common among the Mississippian peoples described by De Soto, De Pratz, and others. My own work with the historic peoples of the Illinois region shows that riverine travel was common, and indeed that the Miamis were considered strange because they weren't known to use canoes (Peregrine 1987:19).

Perhaps a more dramatic example of the extent to which riverine travel was common among the historic peoples of the western Great Lakes comes from the Jesuit missionary Claude Allouez's first meeting with them at Chequamegon Bay in October of 1665. A group of Illinois peoples were there, and explained to Allouez that they had come from the prairies of western Illinois and eastern Iowa to trade with the Chequamegon residents (Thwaites 1896 (50):275; (54):167). They also told Allouez, and later Jacques Marquette, about the great river they lived by (the

Mississippi), and of the peoples who also lived near it as far south as the Gulf of Mexico (Thwaites 1896 (54):185-191; also (59):149,155). From this and other examples that could be offered, it is clear that riverine travel and trade was extensive and important to the historic peoples of the Illinois region, and one can assume it was so for their prehistoric ancestors as well (also see Little 1987).

However, riverine trade may not have been as important to Mississippian societies living south of the Appalachians. There the river systems only allow travel in a generally north-south direction, meaning that east-west travel had to take place, in most cases, overland. Indeed, extensive overland trail systems are well documented for the region (Myer 1928). In the interest of simplicity, then, I will only consider Mississippian site location within the Mississippi River drainage in this analysis.

Assuming rivers to be the major focus of trade in prestige-goods, I can modify Hypothesis Five to suggest that locations within the Mississippi River drainage that could most readily control trade along the river system should have been the locus of Mississippian centers (Peregrine 1991c). The question then becomes one of defining those locations within the Mississippi riverine system that had the highest potential to control trade, and these locations can be readily defined through the graph theoretical concept of centrality.

Graph Theory

Graph theory is a branch of mathematics which examines the properties of graphs and how those properties can elucidate problems in the real world (see Harary 1969:1-7). A graph can be defined simply as a structure consisting of points connected by lines (Hage and Harary 1983:3). If points A and B are connected by a single line, they are said to be adjacent points, and if lines A and B are both incident upon a single point, they are said to be adjacent lines (Harary 1969:9). The degree of a point is the number of lines incident upon it (Harary 1969:14). A walk is an alternating sequence of points and lines, beginning and ending with points, in which each line is incident with the points that proceed and follow it (Harary 1969:13). A walk is called a path if all the points are distinct (Harary 1969:13). The length of a path is the number of lines or steps in it (Hage and Harary 1983:18), and the distance, or geodesic, between two points is the length of the shortest path connecting them (Hage and Harary 1983:18). Finally, the diameter of a graph is the length of the longest geodesic (Harary 1969:14). These are only a few of the most basic terms in graph theory, but they should suffice for the discussion that follows.

A river system, such as the Mississippi, can be easily transformed into a graph. Points are used to represent the sources and junctions of rivers, while lines are used to represent the rivers themselves (Haggett and Chorley 1969). Figure 6.2 shows the Mississippi River system as a graph.

The graph in Figure 6.2 can also be represented by a matrix so that matrix algebra can be used in its analysis. Representing the graph as a matrix allows for an almost unlimited number of algebraic manipulations and analyses to be performed, all of which can be rapidly done on computers (Hage and Harary 1983:101-106; Taffee and Gauthier 1973:116-48). An adjacency matrix can be created by giving the value 1 to cells where the row point and column point are adjacent, and the value 0 where they are not (Hage and Harary 1983:95-96). A distance or geodesic matrix can be created by giving each cell the value of the geodesic between the row and column points (see Hage and Harary 1983:109).

Centrality in a graph has three alternate definitions: (1) as that point in the graph with the highest degree; (2) as that point which falls on the most geodesics between other points; and (3) as that point which is closest to all other points (Freeman 1979:219). Whichever definition is chosen, centrality has been linked to the ability to control the flow of goods and information in exchange networks (Cook et al. 1983:281; Markovsky et al. 1988:220-21), and it is precisely this type of control that I am looking for in the Mississippi River system.

There has been some recent controversy over the use of graph theoretical concepts of centrality for defining control points in exchange networks (Cook et al. 1983; Yamagishi et al. 1988), but most scholars still support their use (Willer 1986; Markovsky et al. 1988), particularly because none of the arguments against using graph theory to predict control points in exchange networks has moved very far away from graph theory. Even Barbara Cook and her colleagues (1983:299-303), who propose a different theoretical framework through which to analyze exchange networks, return in the end to an old graph theoretical idea of vulnerability (see Harary et al. 1965:194-242) to measure centrality, which they admit is basically a measure of betweenness. What these recent debates make clear is that (1) "power and resource distributions depend as much on prevailing exchange conditions as they do on configuration of positions and relations" (Markovsky et al. 1988:232); and (2) "The link between centrality and power is largely intuitive; and the abstract graph-theoretic networks to which these centrality measures have been applied are only loosely coordinated with the social interactive networks they represent" (Cook et al. 1983:289).

What one must recognize is that graph theoretical measures of centrality (degree, betweenness, and closeness) offer a picture of structural centrality only. Deviations from structural centrality should not be looked upon as a failure of graph theory to predict relationships, but rather may offer insights into the particular system in operation. It may be that centrality is not correlated with power in a particular situation, but this is not a failure of graph theory, it is a failure to understand the social relations making up the particular exchange network being studied. Graph theory offers a theoretical "expected" against which to compare observed relations.

There are several good examples of graph theoretical studies in the archaeological literature. Cynthia Irwin-Williams (1977) explained how graph theoretical measures could be used to explore prehistoric settlement in the Puerco River region of northwestern New Mexico. In two influential articles Forrest Pitts (1965, 1978) used graph theory to consider the location of Moscow in terms of its ability to control riverine trade. Mitchell Rothman (1987) employed graph theoretical concepts in a lucid discussion of the interpretation of regional survey data from the Susiana Plain. Rothman (1987:75), in particular, offered a lengthy exploration of graph theory, and argued that it is particularly useful for archaeological analyses because (1) concepts have precise definitions, (2) quantitative features of empirical structures can be readily calculated, and (3) the structure of an observed system can be verified or disconfirmed through logically-derived axioms and theorems (also see Hage and Harary 1983:9). In addition, Rothman (1987:75) explained that graph theory is broadly applicable in terms of its potential subjects, and is therefore a powerful tool for analyzing a wide range of archaeological questions (also see Peregrine 1991c).

A Graph Theoretical Analysis of Mississippian Settlement

Returning to Hypothesis Five, one should find a correlation between positions of high centrality and the locations of Mississippian centers. I will use each of the three measures of centrality mentioned above: (1) degree, (2) betweenness, and (3) closeness. Linton Freeman (1979:221-26) explains that each measure of graph centrality focuses on a different control property:

> The *degree* of a point is viewed as important as an index of its potential *communication activity....Betweenness* is a useful index of the potential of a point for *control* of communication...*closeness*-based indexes of point centrality...may be used when measures based upon *independence* or *efficiency* are desired.

Each of these factors would be related to the ability to control prestige-goods flowing through a particular location, so each measure should have some meaning for Mississippian settlement location.

Freeman (1979:219) defines the degree of a point as "the count of the number of other points...that are adjacent to it and with which it is...in direct contact." A point's degree can be measured by simply counting the number of other points it is in direct contact with (Nieminen 1974). In terms of matrix algebra, this is simply the column sum of the adjacency matrix. Freeman (1979:221) defines the betweenness of a point as "the frequency with which a point falls between pairs of other points on the shortest or geodesic paths connecting them." Measuring betweenness can be

very difficult, particularly for large graphs, but matrix methods for their calculation have been developed (Harary et al. 1965:134-41; Taffee and Gauthier 1973:116-48). Finally, the closeness of a point can be thought of as either "the degree to which it is close to all other points," or as the extent to which "it can avoid the control potential of others" (Freeman 1979:224). The closeness of a point is easily measured "by summing the geodesic distances from that point to all other points in the graph" (Freeman 1979:225; Sabidussi 1966), which is simply the row sum of the geodesic matrix.

The graph used in the analyses that follow is shown in Figure 6.2, and a list of the rivers is given in Table 6.1 (defined by their source and termination

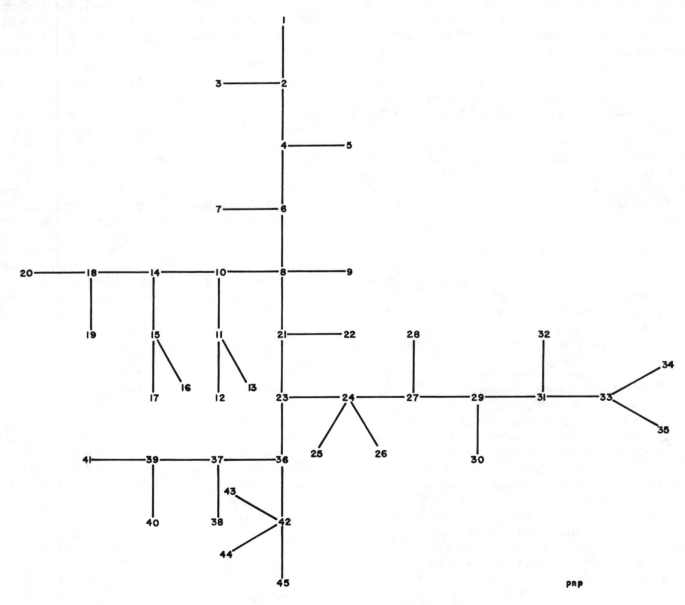

Figure 6.2. Graph of the Mississippi River drainage.

points on the graph). Of course, the choice of rivers that make up this graph could be influential to the outcome of the analyses. I could not include all rivers that are part of the Mississippi drainage, or these analyses would become monstrously complex. A simple cut-off by stream order, size, or the like, would not have been very effective either, as some second-order and small streams are important as transportation routes. I finally decided to use what is effectively an opportunistic sample of the rivers in the Mississippi drainage. The rivers used are those shown in the inset maps of Part I of the *National Water Summary 1985* (USGS 1985). These are the rivers that the United States Geological Survey has identified as the major elements of the Mississippi drainage, so there is some rationale for using them.

Table 6.1. Rivers Shown on Figure 6.2.

Points	River
1 - 45	Mississippi
2 - 3	Minnesota
4 - 5	Wisconsin
6 - 7	Des Moines
8 - 9	Illinois
8 - 20	Missouri
10 - 11	Kansas
11 - 12	Republican
11 - 13	Smoky Hill
14 - 15	Platte
15 - 16	South Fork (Platte)
15 - 17	North Fork (Platte)
18 - 19	Yellowstone
21 - 22	Kaskaskia
23 - 33	Ohio
24 - 25	Tennessee
24 - 26	Cumberland
27 - 28	Wabash
29 - 30	Kentucky
31 - 32	Scioto
33 - 34	Allegheny
33 - 35	Monongahela
36 - 41	Arkansas
37 - 38	Canadian
39 - 40	Cimmarron
42 - 43	Ouachita
42 - 44	Red

Results of the Graph Analyses

Table 6.2 shows the rating of each point in Figure 6.2 on five measures of centrality. Each value has been multiplied by 1000 to convert it into an integer. The first three measures are relative degree (degree / n-1 where n is the number of points in the graph), relative betweenness (betweenness / n-1), and relative closeness (closeness / n-1; with closeness measured inversely so that it becomes larger as a point's closeness to other points increases), all generated by the CENTRALITY procedure in the UCINET GRAPH 3.0 software package (MacEvoy and Freeman 1987).

I also created two new measures of centrality, presented in the last two columns of Table 6.2. The first of these I call geographic closeness. It is simply the row sum of the geodesic matrix, but with the geodesics being measured by the geographic distance between points rather than steps. A graph based upon geographic distances between points is given as Figure 6.3. The values of geographic closeness presented in Table 6.2 are relative measures (geographic closeness / n-1; again with closeness measured inversely). The final measure of centrality is what I call geographic degree. I created this measure by weighting each line incident upon a point by the inverse of its length, summing these weights, and multiplying by the degree of the point:

Equation 6.1: $P = (\Sigma (1/L)) * D$

Where:

L = length of a path incident on point P

D = the degree of point P

The multiplier D is used simply to make the range of possible values greater.

Lines incident on point P which are long, under Equation 6.1, are given less weight than lines which are short. Since degree is a measure of communication activity, it makes sense that if a point is far away the potential to communicate with it is lower than if the point were closer. Geographic degree is simply an expression of this idea, giving greater weight to communication potential with points that are closer than those that are more distant. Again, this measure is presented as a relative one (geographic degree / n-1).

It is interesting to note that the correlation between closeness and geographic closeness for this graph is 0.856, and the correlation for degree and geographic degree is 0.868 (computed from a regression analysis using the PLOT procedure in SPSSX [SPSS, Inc. 1988]). These strong correlations suggest that it is not necessary to take "real world" conditions into account when measuring centrality in this graph. Weighting

Table 6.2. Point Scores on Five Measures of Centrality.

Point	Scores					Point	Scores				
	RB[a]	RC[b]	RD[c]	GC[d]	GD[e]		RB[a]	RC[b]	RD[c]	GC[d]	GD[e]
01	0	137	23	51	6	26	0	190	23	60	3
02	90	158	68	65	74	27	312	205	68	89	104
03	0	137	23	54	8	28	0	171	23	67	4
04	172	184	68	75	74	29	246	179	68	76	80
05	0	156	23	57	6	30	0	152	23	62	8
06	246	216	68	87	70	31	172	157	68	68	91
07	0	178	23	61	4	32	0	136	23	60	11
08	603	254	91	101	197	33	90	138	68	58	114
09	0	204	23	78	8	34	0	121	23	49	8
10	382	224	68	78	91	35	0	121	23	54	23
11	90	187	68	75	62	36	354	229	68	81	57
12	0	158	23	59	6	37	172	194	68	68	98
13	0	158	23	53	4	38	0	163	23	43	2
14	251	194	68	80	64	39	90	165	68	70	92
15	90	165	68	65	51	40	0	142	23	53	6
16	0	142	23	50	6	41	0	142	23	21	2
17	0	142	23	46	4	42	133	192	91	64	75
18	90	165	68	47	23	43	0	162	23	70	4
19	0	142	23	36	3	44	0	162	23	35	2
20	0	142	23	31	2	45	0	162	23	54	8
21	532	262	68	100	170						
22	0	209	23	83	11		[a] Relative betweenness.				
23	638	263	68	101	153		[b] Relative closeness.				
24	404	234	91	100	208		[c] Relative degree.				
25	0	190	23	60	3		[d] Geographic closeness.				
							[e] Geographic degree.				

these measures by distance created very little variation in the outcome of the analyses. Whether this is true with other graphs is beyond the scope of this work, but similar correlations should not be surprising if one remembers that these are measures of the basic structure of a graph, and although geographic weighting may change various elements of the graph, the graph as a whole and as a structure will not dramatically change (compare Figures 6.2 and 6.3).

Table 6.3 presents the points of the graph in Figure 6.2 ranked in order of their summed scores on the five measures of centrality. Because of the variability in the scores presented in Table 6.1, this ranking should not be taken as distinct. The rankings change depending on which measure is used and what method is employed to depict centrality relationships. It is clear, however, that four points (8, 21, 23, and 24) stand out in each measure, and that three additional points (10, 27, and 36) are also relatively central. With this information I constructed a "zone of centrality"

on the graph in Figure 6.2. This zone is shown in Figure 6.4.

The Location of Mississippian Centers

Going back again to Hypothesis Five, one should expect major Mississippian centers to be located in the zone of centrality. Outside of this zone, one should expect there to be fewer Mississippian centers. If Mississippian centers are located outside of this zone, their positioning should be explainable in terms of the functioning Mississippian prestige-good system.

Figure 6.5 shows the locations of major Mississippian centers in the Mississippi River drainage. These are not, by any means, all Mississippian sites that are consistent with Bruce Smith's definition of "center," as given in the last chapter. There are hundreds of such "centers" in the Mississippi Valley, and including all of them would have not only necessitated a formidable literature and museum search,

Table 6.3. Point Ranks Based on Five
Measures of Centrality.

Point	Total	Point	Total
8	1246	26	276
23	1196	7	266
21	1132	28	265
24	1037	43	259
10	848	45	247
36	789	12	246
27	778	30	245
6	687	5	242
29	649	13	238
14	657	32	230
37	600	40	224
4	573	3	222
31	556	44	222
42	555	16	221
39	485	35	221
11	482	1	217
33	468	17	215
2	455	41	208
15	439	19	204
18	393	38	204
22	326	34	201
9	313	20	198
25	276		

but would have turned the figure into a dot collage worthy of Seurat. I selected the twenty-eight sites shown in the figure from the following articles and books: Brain (1978), Brose (1978), Brown et al. (1978), Essenpreis (1978), Fowler and Hall (1978), Griffin (1978a, 1978b), Harn (1978), Kneberg (1952), Mason (1981), Morse and Morse (1983), Muller (1978, 1986), and Price (1978), if the author thought them to be the major center for a particular region. There is great diversity in the complexity of these sites, their sizes, and the lengths of their occupations, but they do represent, I think, a reasonable sample of major regional Mississippian centers in the Mississippi River drainage.

There is an obvious correlation with the location of many of the centers shown on Figure 6.5 and the zone of centrality. Cahokia, specifically, the major Mississippian center in the entire region, is located directly on point 8, one of the points exhibiting highest centrality (see Peregrine 1991). More than a third of these centers (11 of 28) are in or near the zone of centrality. The centers which are not in this zone tend to cluster towards it—in other words, there are very few centers near the edges of the graph. Figure 6.5 appears to support Hypothesis Five.

However, several Mississippian centers, and indeed two major groupings of centers, are located outside of the zone of centrality. The first deviant group is located in eastern Tennessee. All of these are situated at the far southeastern edge of the graph, adjacent to the Appalachians. This location is ideal for carrying on trade across the mountains with groups in the southeast Mississippian heartland. Indeed, there is good evidence that these centers had strong and continuing ties with southeastern Mississippian groups throughout the entire Mississippian period (Lewis and Kneberg 1946; Schroedl 1986; Polhemus 1987). The location of this group of centers, and perhaps the somewhat deviant locations of the two centers above them on the Tennessee River, can be explained in terms of trade across the Appalachians.

Another group of deviant centers is located along the Illinois River. These are, in general, poorly documented sites, and it has been suggested that they were not contemporaneous (Harn 1978:245). None of them are very large, and it may have been that these centers were built in succession through time (Harn 1978:246-47). Even if this clustering of centers is a temporal phenomena, one must still explain what made the central Illinois River valley produce so many centers. One reason is certainly that the environment was quite favorable to the Mississippian means of production (Harn 1978:244), but another could be that the Illinois River forms a major link between the Great Lakes and the Mississippi River, specifically with Cahokia. The Illinois River links Cahokia and the rest of the central Mississippi Valley with Canada and the Northeast over a very short portage on the Des Plains River near Chicago. The only other short portages linking the Great Lakes with the Mississippi occur on the Fox River in Wisconsin, and downstream from these one finds the centers of Aztalan and Apple River (depending on the portages and rivers chosen). Trade with Canada and the Northeast may explain the location of these deviant centers.

Two other deviant regions are not so easily dealt with, but this is no surprise as both are enigmatic Mississippian regions to being with. One is the Caddoan area in Arkansas and Oklahoma, and specifically the Spiro site (Brown et al. 1978). The other is the Fort Ancient region in Ohio, and specifically the Baum site (Griffin 1978a). Both are classic Mississippian centers, yet are isolated from the central Mississippian region. They are not located on clearly advantageous trade routes either, as, for example, Aztalan is. Neither has been sufficiently investigated, so information about them is insufficient for a detailed analysis.

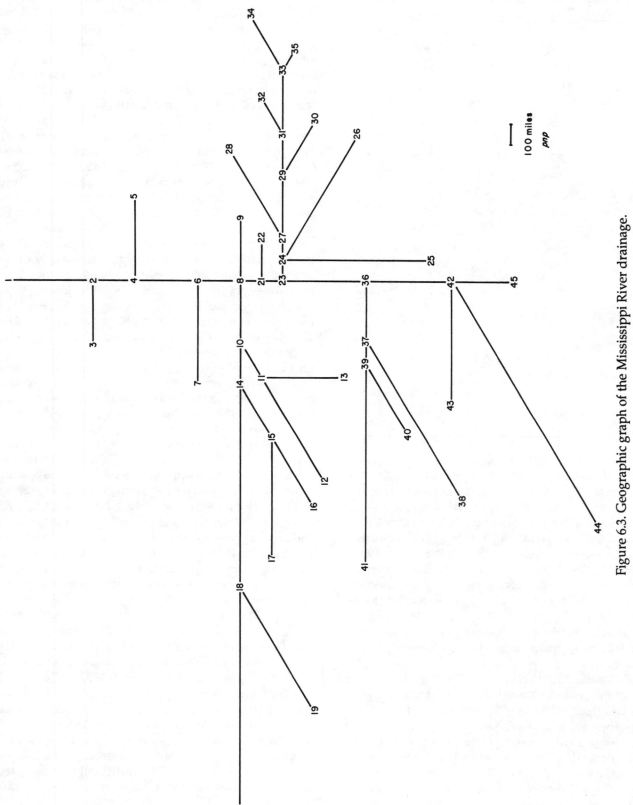

Figure 6.3. Geographic graph of the Mississippi River drainage.

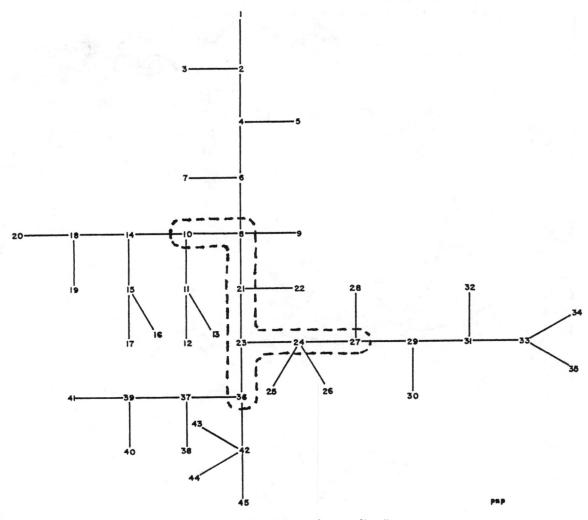

Figure 6.4. The "zone of centrality."

It does appear, however, that both Spiro and Baum are centers for integrated, marginal Mississippian societies, which are linked to the Mississippian system yet separate from it. Certainly prestige-goods flowed into and out of the Caddoan and Fort Ancient regions: Spiro boasts the greatest concentration of worked shell in North America (Phillips and Brown 1978) and Fort Ancient sites yield large numbers of Mississippian prestige-goods (Griffin 1978a). These sites, however, may have been responding to factors other than the control of trade, as their locations cannot be easily explained with this model.

Despite the enigmatic nature of the Caddoan and Fort Ancient regions, Hypothesis Five appears to be supported. Many Mississippian centers are located in the zone of centrality, including the major center Cahokia, located at the point of highest centrality in the system. The location of centers situated outside of this zone can be readily explained in terms of trade with peripheral areas. It appears that trade in pres-

tige-goods played an important role in the location of Mississippian centers.

Conclusions

In this chapter I have presented evidence to support the idea that both trade in prestige-goods and the ability to monopolistically control prestige-goods played important roles in the political evolution of Mississippian societies. Mississippian political centers were located where riverine trade could be readily controlled, suggesting that trade held an important political function in Mississippian societies. Prestige-goods used by the Mississippian peoples changed over time, becoming more exotic and ornate, and more easy to control. This suggests that the ability to control prestige-goods also held an important political function in Mississippian societies. Both ideas support the basic premise examined in this chapter, that a prestige-good system was an active force in

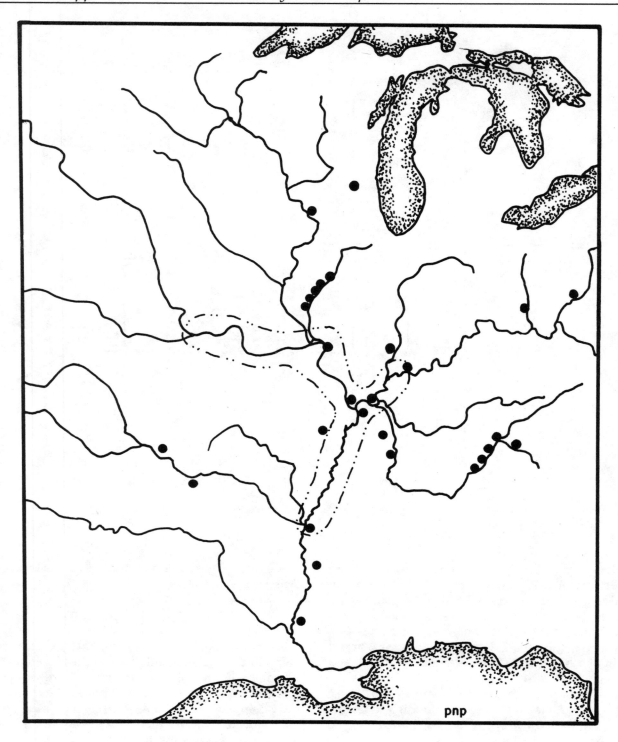

Figure 6.5. Mississippian centers and the "zone of centrality."

Mississippian evolution Now that I have demonstrated that a prestige-good system was present during the Mississippian period, and that the system apparently played an important role in Mississippian social evolution, I can turn to the fundamental problem of this work: developing a new theory of Mississippian social evolution.

7

Conclusions

Summary of the Work

In Chapter 1 I introduced the basic problem of Mississippian evolution, and outlined previous theories of Mississippian evolution. These theories were of two basic types: (1) contact/migration, and (2) in-situ development. I argued that contact/migration theories have little explanatory power, and that theories of in-situ development, focused generally on agriculture, warfare, or population growth as "prime movers" for Mississippian evolution, are problematic as well. I suggested a new theory of Mississippian evolution, based upon the world-system perspective, and focused on inter-regional trade in exotic goods and its underlying social structure as a force behind the evolution of Mississippian societies.

In Chapter 2 I developed the basic model of a world-system based upon trade in exotic goods. I adapted the model from the ideas of Claude Meillassoux, who suggested that in some societies lineage elders maintain their power by controlling access to exotic goods needed for social reproduction (initiation, brideprice, funerary, and other social payments), and Kajsa Ekholm, who suggested that political power in the Kongo Kingdom was based upon the control of prestige-goods. From these two ideas I developed the model of a prestige-good system (a world-system based upon a division of labor in prestige-goods), and offered three ethnographic examples: Kongo, Tonga, and Karavar.

In Chapter 3 I considered how political centralization occurs prestige-good systems, and how these systems evolve. I argued that the power of political leaders in these systems is tied to the "trade density" of prestige-goods, and that trade density, in turn, is the product of the system's population and the volume of trade. I suggested that political power fluctuates as these two variables fluctuate. I discussed three ethnographic cases that supported the model: the Kwakiutl, the Kiriwina Islanders, and the Medieval Catholic church. Finally, I suggested that prestige-good systems evolve out of a corporate lineage structure in situations where lineage elders cannot control the means of production, and so attempt to control the means of social reproduction.

In Chapter 4 I considered prestige-goods themselves, in order to determine which goods in the material record of Mississippian societies might have been prestige-goods. I searched the Standard Cross-Cultural Sample of 186 societies in order to identify potential prestige-good systems. I located a total of 27 prestige-good systems, and coded 132 prestige-goods used in these systems. I then analyzed the goods using descriptive statistics and cluster analysis, and defined four general categories of prestige-goods: (1) furs, (2) bead goods, (3) small, durable personal ornaments, and (4) large, complex personal ornaments of less durable materials. I compared the prestige-goods used in societies of differing political centralization and demonstrated that more politically centralized societies used more exotic and ornate prestige-goods than less politically centralized societies. I suggested that political leaders in prestige-good systems actively select more complex goods as they gain power, because these goods are easier to control.

In Chapter 5 I presented and tested three hypotheses in order to determine if a Mississippian prestige-good system existed. Hypothesis One was that political centers should have more prestige-goods than peripheral areas. Hypothesis Two was that adult males should have more prestige-goods than either juveniles or females. Hypothesis Three was that the falloff of prestige-goods from centers should not form a distribution suggestive of free exchange. I tested these hypothesis with burial data from the American Bottom in Illinois, and the Tellico Reservoir region in eastern Tennessee. Although the available data were barely sufficient, all three hypotheses were supported by the archaeological record, and I concluded that a prestige-good system likely existed during the Mississippian period. I also discussed Paul Welch's (1986, 1991) analysis of the Moundville chiefdom, which supported this conclusion.

In Chapter 6 I continued to evaluate the Mississippian material record, in order to determine if the proposed Mississippian prestige-good system had any influence on Mississippian evolution, and tested two additional hypotheses. Hypothesis Four was that prestige-goods should have become more exotic and ornate as Mississippian societies became more politically centralized. Hypothesis Five was that political centers should have emerged in places where trade in prestige-goods could be readily controlled. I found strong support in the archaeological record for Hypothesis Four. A graph theoretical analysis suggested that Mississippian centers tended to be located where riverine trade could be controlled, supporting Hypothesis Five. I concluded that the control of prestige-goods was a significant factor in Mississippian social evolution.

Mississippian Evolution

The summary above brings me to the denouement of this work: a new theory of Mississippian evolution. I have shown how prestige-good systems operate, that Mississippian societies functioned within the framework of a prestige-good system, and that the processes of this prestige-good system were an active force in the evolution of Mississippian societies. I have also developed and evaluated a model of social evolution in prestige-good systems, and I can now pull these ideas together into a verifiable statement on Mississippian evolution.

The way in which the Mississippian prestige-good system initially came into existence is perhaps the most difficult question to answer in this framework. In Chapter 3 I developed a general theory for the evolution of prestige-good systems. I suggested that prestige-good systems evolve from a corporate lineage structure in situations where lineage elders cannot readily control the means of production. In these situations, elders employ symbols of office and esoteric knowledge about the supernatural to control younger members of the lineage, who must align themselves with an elder in order to socially reproduce (Meillassoux 1978). Elders supply youths with knowledge and ritual insignia so that they can be initiated, get married, take office in the lineage, and the like. It is from the power elders gain through their control of ritual insignia that a prestige-good system first begins.

In eastern North America, corporate lineage structure appears to be present at least as far back as the Archaic period. Charles and Buikstra (1983) argue that burial mounds began to be constructed during the Late Archaic period as symbols of lineage membership and control of specific territories. Certainly elders in these lineages could not have readily controlled the means of production, as hunting and gathering are not easily regulated. An alternate strategy for these elders to gain power would have been to initiate the use of objects and knowledge that they uniquely controlled in ceremonies of social reproduction (Meillassoux 1978:138). It is an interesting fact that at this time trade in particular exotic goods began (Winters 1968). I suggest that the Late Archaic period saw the initiation of a prestige-good system that would, over time, evolve into Mississippian societies.

A very similar case is made by Barbara Bender (1985a, 1985b) to explain the shift from hunter-gatherer to horticulturalist in eastern North America. For the Archaic period Bender's (1985a) argument parallels that given above. For the Woodland period Bender (1985b:39-40) offers a detailed and lucid discussion of what appears to be a prestige-good system in the American midcontinent:

> the more intensive and extensive ceremonialism of the late Early and Middle Woodland must reflect an important sphere of ritual mediation and locus of authority...the role of certain individuals as ritual mediators is...made visible in the burial paraphernalia.

These burial paraphernalia are prestige-goods: "[copper] earspools, breast plates, mica mirrors, conch shells, rattles and pipes" (Bender 1985b:40). Bender (1985b:41) suggests that there existed a direct link between prestige-goods and political power in these Woodland societies:

> leaders continued and greatly elaborated...material manipulation. The prestigious grave goods...suggests that certain individuals controlled access to exotic raw materials and particularly fine local materials, and to specific items such as blocked-end tubular pipes, large bifacial points, gorgets, boatstones, cones, and beads.

Bender (1985b:43) goes on to explain that "raw materials and prestige items seem to have been used for...display and ritual offering. They are insignia of position. But they were also used for exchange between neighboring elites."

These prestige-goods may have been used by Woodland elites to arrange marriages between localized lineage groups. Biodistance analyses of Woodland populations demonstrate marked differences in biodistance between males and females. Females in a given Middle Woodland community tend to be more closely related to individuals in other communities than males are, suggesting that females were circulating as connubia between communities with relatively stable male populations (Droessler 1981:165). Prestige-goods may have also been a means by which local elites mediated territorial arrangements with neighboring elites (Brose 1979), and it certainly appears that Middle Woodland elites used prestige-goods to display status (Bender 1985b; Buikstra 1976:29-32).

The distribution and use of prestige-goods that Bender describes gives a strong indication that a prestige-good system was operating during the Middle Woodland period. Indeed Bender (1985b:46) suggests that Woodland societies could have been structured something like those of the historic Northwest Coast, which were, as discussed in Chapter 3, participants in a prestige-good system. Bender (1985b:47) even states that in order to maintain social prestige and political power in Woodland societies, there was a "need to amass quantities of exotica." Woodland societies appear to have been participants in some form of a prestige-good system.

The processes through which the Mississippian prestige-good system evolved out of this Woodland system are not entirely clear. Prior to the Mississippian emergence the Woodland prestige-good system declined. Burial ceremonialism decreased, the territorial, riverine settlement pattern was replaced by a more dispersed one, and (perhaps most importantly from my perspective) the "Hopewell Interaction Sphere," by which exotic prestige-goods moved through the midcontinent, disappeared, although trade in shell and other less exotic prestige-goods continued (Droessler 1981:12). Despite the arguments several scholars have made (particularly Braun and Plog 1983; Buikstra 1976; and Styles 1981), that there is social continuity between the Middle and Late Woodland periods, it seems to me that the disappearance of elaborate burial ceremonialism, alterations in settlement patterns, and decline of inter-regional trade in exotic goods are evidence of important social changes taking place, changes that need to be carefully investigated rather than ignored.

Joseph Tainter (1977a, 1977b, 1983) suggests that these social changes were brought about by the dissolution of the highest level of the Middle Woodland political hierarchy. He argues that Late Woodland societies became organized at a lower hierarchical level, probably at the level of corporate lineages. These lineages dispersed across the landscape and practiced a different pattern of social interaction than the riverine-based one of Middle Woodland societies. These new patterns of social structure and interaction must have underlain the Mississippian prestige-good system, and it is unfortunate that they are not more completely understood.

The Woodland-Mississippian transition seems to be broadly characterized by an increase in societal scale, complexity, and integration. In the context of a prestige-good system, an increase in societal scale would reflect an increased ability of political leaders to control the distribution of prestige-goods over wider ranges, and mechanisms to maintain control could result in increases in complexity and integration. The new patterns of social organization and interaction that appeared in the Late Woodland period may have fostered competition between elites and encouraged social changes that increased their control over flows of prestige-goods. It is difficult, given the small quantity and poor quality of available data, to precisely describe the changes that took place, but I hypothesize that they may have included the development of sumptuary rules restricting consumption of higher-order goods to elites, new mechanisms of labor control for the manufacture and transportation of prestige-goods, and perhaps new forms of political structure or alliance for solidifying the control of trade routes.

Although the social changes that accompanied the Woodland-Mississippian transition are not clear, the stage was apparently set for the re-emergence of higher-order political leaders in the emergent Mississippian period. Once the emergent Mississippian prestige-good system, which included new social structures allowing political leaders greater control over prestige-goods, came into operation, I suggest that Mississippian evolution followed the model presented in Chapter 1, developed in Chapter 3, and tested in Chapter 6. Mississippian societies represent increasing political centralization, and under the model this should be caused by decreasing trade density. Decreasing trade density, in turn, is the product of three interacting variables: (1) population, (2) trade volume, and (3) system boundedness.

The initial emergence of Mississippian societies brought about no obvious change in trade volume, and the prestige-good system had apparently rather open boundaries during the entire Mississippian period (Helmkamp 1985). Population, however, apparently rose during the Late Woodland period (Buikstra 1977:76-77, 81; Muller 1978:302, 1986:138, 146, 148; Morse and Morse 1983:202, 214). Buikstra and her colleagues (1986, 1987) argue that this population increase was due to an increase in fertility, and may have been tied to the hypothesized social changes discussed above. Elites may have promoted a population increase in their sphere of influence in order to create a large labor pool for the manufacture and transportation of prestige-goods, and perhaps for the conquest or defense of important trade routes (Nag, White, and Peet 1978).

With a relatively stable flow of prestige-goods, and a growing population desiring them for social reproduction, trade density would have declined, and the power of elites controlling prestige-goods would have increased proportionally. Although some might be dissatisfied with this model, arguing that it is simply another version of the "population pressure" models I argued against in Chapter 1, I suggest that it is not. Population here is not assumed to be a "prime mover," but is only active relative to other variables, and only fosters cultural change in the specific social circumstances of a prestige-good system.

Within this intensifying prestige-good system, elites advantageously located on the riverine trade network, and having a social structure in place to be able to control trade through this advantageous location, would have had better access to prestige-goods, and would have gained power accordingly (Brown et al. 1990; Steponaitis 1991). Of course, advantageous location must have included access to rich alluvial soils which were suitable to intensified production through maize horticulture (Ward 1965; Peebles 1978; Steponaitis 1991:195) to support political personnel specializing in trade and manufacture of prestige-goods. Population would have been drawn to these more powerful elites, decreasing trade density locally, and in turn increasing the power of these elites and further differentiating them from the rest of society. Thus social stratification, population concentration, and a reliance on maize horticulture emerged as core/periphery differentiation in the Mississippian prestige-good system became more pronounced.

Mississippian evolution in this framework is not the product of a single "prime mover," but rather the product of interrelated processes, including core/periphery differentiation between advantageously located populations and others, competition between elites to affirm or increase their power and prestige, and to provide their followers with better opportunities to socially reproduce, technological innovations in food and craft production, and population growth, all acting withing a feedback relationship with one another. Within the framework of an existing prestige-good system, which had been present in the Eastern Woodlands since the Archaic period, lineage elders able to control trade in prestige-goods were also able to gain power. Social change during the Middle Woodland period led to corporate lineages as the basic social, economic, and political unit, creating and legitimating lineage heads as primary sociopolitical leaders within the framework of this existing prestige-good system. These social changes led to increased levels of competition over access to prestige-goods, and may have fostered population growth. Innovations in food production allowed for the centralization of population and authority at nodal points on trade routes, and allowed political leaders to support artisans who created ornate goods for the prestige-good system. Core/periphery differentiation and competition between core elites fostered continued centralization of political power, culminating in Mississippian societies as we know them archaeologically.

The Nature of Mississippian Societies

Having shown that Mississippian societies were participating in a prestige-good system and that their evolution was closely linked to the processes of that system, I am in a unique position to describe some of the political, economic, and social structures that must have been present in Mississippian societies. This is one of the most exciting elements of the prestige-good system model. Because it was generated and supported with ethnographic data, I can use the conclusions reached in Chapter 2 concerning the nature of societies participating in prestige-good systems to make some definitive statements on the nature of Mississippian societies (Peregrine 1991a).

In terms of political organization, the implications of the Mississippian prestige-good system are obvious. Political power was based upon the ability to control prestige-goods, legitimated through a lineage structure. Since Mississippian societies were apparently organized as chiefdoms, there was likely a hierarchy of chiefs, similar perhaps to Kongo and Tonga, with the pre-eminent chief located at a major center, and lower level chiefs located at minor centers and in outlying hamlets. This kind of hierarchical arrangement seems to be reflected in some Mississippian settlement systems (Fowler 1978; but cf. Milner 1990). The political hierarchy itself was probably organized like a lineage, with individuals in each level both superior and socially "elder" to individuals in levels below them (DePratter 1983:100-10). At the lowest level in the political hierarchy were localized lineages, with elder males as their heads.

Ancestry would have been the most important element in the ideological system that supported this form of political organization. A "cult of the ancestors" in some form was likely present in Mississippian societies, and seems to be reflected in the elaborate burial ceremonializm characteristic of Mississippian societies (DePratter 1983:111-54). The pre-eminent chief himself was probably both the social and spiritual "father" of the chiefdom. He was seen as a contact between the ancestors and the people, as he was the social elder of the people, and so the closest to the ancestors (DePratter 1983:86). Therefore, the pre-eminent chief's closeness to the ancestors would have reinforced his political authority (Shils 1971).

Localized corporate lineages would have formed the basic social structure in Mississippian societies, as seems to be reflected in the layout of some Mississippian cemeteries (Goldstein 1980:136-37). Lineage leaders were the "socially" eldest members of the lineage. Social age was likely a dual product of one's ancestry and one's ability to create alliances with elder lineage members (Meillassoux 1978). There were probably a number of ritual grades in Mississippian societies, some of which were necessary to simply be recognized as an adult or as a member of the society, and some in which membership brought prestige and political power (Hudson 1976:325-27, 336-40).

Finally, localized lineages would have also been the basic economic units in Mississippian societies. Women and juvenile females took care of most day-to-day economic activities, while young men were probably most concerned with serving elder males from whom they could obtain prestige-goods. Some individuals apparently served as craftsmen, manufacturing prestige-goods for pre-eminent chiefs located at major riverine centers (Welch 1986:171-72). There may have been specialized long-distance traders at major centers as well, and who also served the pre-eminent chief. Although horticulture was practiced in order to produce enough to both support these individuals and allow them to remain in the same location, there was probably little systematic trade between centers and outlying hamlets in maize or other agricultural products (Welch 1986:120-32; cf. Dincauze and Hasenstab 1989; O'Brien 1990). The logistics of bulk trade in the Mississippian period would have been great, and major centers were located on rich soils, certainly capable of producing enough to support the inhabitants (Peebles 1978).

Recommendations for Future Work

It seems obvious that we need more data before we can expand and refine the study of the Mississippian prestige-good system. The simple fact is that Midwestern archaeologists must start publishing more data. There is no excuse for the situation, so evident in the research presented here, that many simple analyses one might want to perform on archaeological data from the Midwest is impossible because the data are not readily obtainable. Research into Archaic and Woodland systems also needs to be initiated in order to better understand the evolution of the Mississippian prestige-good system. The Hopewellian period offers an exciting prospect for applying the theory developed here to the evolution (and collapse) of another complex society in eastern North America. A work similar to this one, but focusing on the Hopewellian prestige-good system, could be a significant project. More research into Archaic trade should provide evidence of similar processes at work, and may add insights into the origin of these indigenous world-systems.

A second area for future research concerns the theory itself. As it exists now, the theory is almost completely top-down in nature; that is, cultural evolution is seen to stem from the actions of elites, and little emphasis is given to the motivations of non-elites. Additional work in world-systems theory needs to be done to better understand why individuals would "buy into" the prestige-good system. Indeed, the entire theory needs to be better linked to world-systems theory in general, specifically to more recent work on pre-capitalist and non-capitalist world-systems (for example Abu-Lughod 1989; Chase-Dunn and Hall 1991; Rowlands, Larson and Kristiansen 1987).

However, if the waxing and waning of prestige-good systems characterize social evolution in the Archaic, Woodland, and Mississippian periods, then a significant theoretical breakthrough may be imminent in Midwestern archaeology. An encompassing framework, which explains processes occurring throughout most of eastern North American prehistory will be available, and with it the potential to tie cultural evolution in eastern North America together in a unified theoretical perspective. Work I have in progress suggests that indigenous world-systems existed at the time of European contact (Peregrine 1989a), and that cultural change in the historic period can be understood in the framework of world-system contact (Peregrine 1988, 1989a). I believe the most important avenue for future research is to pursue the world-system perspective, and attempt to create through it a unified perspective on cultural evolution in eastern North America. I hope this work has provided a first step towards that goal.

Appendix A: Annotated Codebook for the Prestige-Goods Study

Appendix A. Annotated Codebook for the Prestige-Goods Study.			
Cols.	Var.	Description	
1-4	ID	Identification number	
5	B1	Blank	
6	PMT	Primary material type	
		1-plant	6-stone
		2-animal	7-precious stone
		3-clay	8-other
		4-metal	9-unknown/none
		5-precious metal	
7	PMO	Primary material origin	
		1-local	
		2-non-local	
		9-unknown/none	
8	SMT	Secondary material type	
9	SMO	Secondary material origin	
10	TMT	Tertiary material type	
11	TMO	Tertiary material origin	
12	B2	Blank	
13	CLASS	Object class	
		1-personal ornament	5-weapon
		2-household ornament	8-other
		3-ritual object	9-unknown
		4-utensil	
14	FUNC	Object functionality	
		1-functional	9-unknown
		2-non-functional	
15	USE	Object use	
		1-used	9-unknown
		2-not used	
16	AGE	Object age	
		1-new	4-composite
		2-antique	9-unknown
		3-either	
17	B3	Blank	
18	FORM	Gross form	
		1-ovoid	5-animorphic
		2-rectanguloid	6-anthropomorphic
		3-complex geometric	8-other
		4-composite	9-unknown
19	PC	Primary color	
		1-clear/none	6-blue
		2-white/silver	7-black
		3-red	8-brown/tan
		4-yellow/gold	9-unknown
		5-green	

Continued

Cols.	Var.	Description	
		Appendix A. Continued	
20	SC	Secondary color	
21	TC	Tertiary color	
22	PD	Primary decoration	
		1-none	5-inlaid/appliqued
		2-painted	8-other
		3-incised/embossed	9-unknown
		4-carved/shaped	
23	SD	Secondary decoration	
24	TD	Tertiary decoration	
25	PDF	Primary design form	
		1-none	4-anthropomorphic
		2-geometric	9-unknown
		3-animorphic	
26	SDF	Secondary design form	
27	TDF	Tertiary design form	
28	FIN	Gross finish	
		1-natural	4-composite
		2-unfinished	9-unknown
		3-finished	
29	SURF	Surface characteristics	
		1-rough	4-composite
		2-smooth	9-unknown
		3-polished	
30	SIZE	Object gross size	
		1-small (LT 10cm3)	4-small or medium
		2-medium (10cm3<>100cm3)	5-medium or large
		3-large (GT 100cm3)	9-unknown
31	B4	Blank	
32	ACQ	Acquisition labor	
		1-low	3-high
		2-moderate	9-unknown
33	MAN	Manufacturing labor	
		--use same values as ACQ	
34	DUR	Durability	
		--use same values as ACQ	
35	APP	Appearance	
		1-natural	4-extravagant
		2-ordinary	9-unknown
		3-extraordinary	
36	B5	Blank	

Continued

Appendix A. Continued

Cols.	Var.	Description		
37	SEXRES	Sex restrictions on possession of object		
		1-none	3-females only	
		2-males only	9-unknown	
38	AGERES	Age restrictions on possession of object		
		1-none	5-youths only	
		2-elders only	6-other/combination	
		3-eldest only	9-unknown	
		4-adults only		
39	SOCRES	Social restrictions on possession of object		
		1-none	5-lowest status only	
		2-high status only	8-other/combination	
		3-highest status only	9-unknown	
		4-low status only		
40	RITRES	Ritual restrictions on possession of object		
		1-none	5-political office	
		2-initiates only	holders only	
		3-priests/shamans only	8-other/combination	
		4-ritual office holders only	9-unknown	
41	B6	Blank		
42	EXCH	Is object typically exchanged		
		1-never	4-always	
		2-sometimes	9-unknown	
		3-often		
43	FOR	Object typically exchanged for		
		1-not applicable	5-human	
		2-another object (same type)	8-other/combination	
		3-another object (different type)	9-unknown	
		4-food		
44	COST	Typical cost of exchange		
		1-not applicable	5-exchanged for item of lower value	
		2-no pattern		
		3-exchanged for item of equal value	8-no basis for comparison	
		4-exchanged for item of greater value	9-unknown	
45	WHO	Who typically gives/receives object		
		1-no pattern	5-between levels (either 2 or 3)	
		2-superior to inferior		
		3-inferior to superior	9-unknown	
		4-same level		
46	REL	Typical relationship of giver/receiver		
		1-no pattern	4-relative	
		2-foreigner	9-unknown	
		3-local		

Continued

Cols.	Var.	Description	
47	B7	Blank	
48	CHAR	Social characteristics of object	
		1-none	5-political symbol
		2-status symbol	6-combination
		3-age symbol	8-other
		4-ritual symbol	9-unknown
49	POW	Power inherent in object	
		1-none	4-dangerous for those
		2-for anyone who possesses it	who cannot control it
		3-for those with knowledge to	8-other
		use it	9-unknown
50	TAB	Taboos surrounding object's misuse/abuse	
		1-none	4-severe
		2-slight	9-unknown
		3-moderate	
51	PUN	Punishment for object's misuse/abuse	
		1-none	4-severe
		2-slight	9-unknown
		3-moderate	
52	DES	Is object destroyed or modified	
		1-never	5-sometimes modified
		2-sometimes	6-often modified
		3-often	7-always modified
		4-always	9-unknown
53	B8	Blank	
54	WHE	Where object is primarily located	
		1-no specific area	4-in village
		2-in dwelling	communal area
		3-in ceremonial	5-outside village
		structure/area	8-other
			9-unknown
55	DIS	How is object disposed of	
		1-never deliberately	4-alone far from
		2-with household/village	houshold/village
		garbage	8-no pattern
		3-alone in/near	9-unknown
		household/village	
56	GRA	Is object placed in grave of owner	
		1-never	4-always
		2-sometimes	9-unknown
		3-often	
57	B9	Blank	
58-60	SCCS	Standard Cross-Cultural Sample number for society	

Appendix A. Continued

Annotations For Selected Variables

PMT,SMT,TMT. Occasionally the raw material or materials used in manufacturing goods were not specifically mentioned. For PMT I generally guessed, as best I could. I sometimes guessed for SMT and TMT if I had a good clue for what the material was. For example, the string in a string of shell beads from Oceania could be assumed to be made of plant material, even if not specifically stated to be so, and I would code it as plant rather than unknown. There are only a few cased in which I guessed, however, and most were similar to the above example.

PMO,SMO,TMO. Materials were assumed to be of local origin if they could be found locally and it was not specifically stated that they were from non-local sources. If there was no mention of them being of non-local origin and I was uncertain if the material was available locally, the material's origin was coded as unknown.

CLASS. Raw materials including furs and bolts of cloth were coded as 8 (other). Any object having to do with warfare, including defensive paraphernalia such as shields, were coded as 5 (weapon).

FUNC. An object was considered functional if it could be utilized for its apparent purpose.

USED. Objects were considered to be used if they were functional and it was not specifically stated that they were not used.

AGE. Raw materials were assumed to be new unless specifically stated otherwise, as were goods that would degrade quickly, such as feathers. Composite goods were those with both new and antique materials as part of them.

FORM. Form refers to the gross form of an object. An animal effigy pipe would be coded as having an animorphic gross form and not an animorphic primary design form. Cylinders were considered rectanguloid rather than ovoid. Strings of beads were considered ovoid, even if the beads were square. Complex geometric means that there are only geometric elements to the form. Composite means that there are non-geometric elements, which could be natural shapes or animorphic or anthropomorphic forms. Raw materials and other naturally shaped goods, such as furs, were coded as 8 (other). Cloth and blankets were coded 2 (rectanguloid).

PC,SC,TC. Items referred to as single-color goods, such as "red walking stick", were coded as having only a primary color, even through they may have had some secondary color. If I was uncertain whether there was a secondary or tertiary color, the object was coded with 9 (unknown) for each. In some cases I assumed that there were no secondary or tertiary colors, as in the case above, and coded with 1 (none) for each.

PD,SD,TD. Decoration is work done in addition to the object's gross form. As explained above, an animal effigy pipe would be coded as having an animorphic gross form and no primary, secondary, or tertiary decoration. If geometric designs were incised into the animal effigy, then the object would be coded as having an incised (3) primary decoration. If an object had other objects tied to it, it was coded as having an appliqued (5) decoration.

PDF,SDF,TDF. These were coded similarly to FORM.

FIN. An object's finish often had to be inferred from the description. It was assumed that an object had been finished unless it was specifically stated that it had been left unfinished.

SURF. Surface characteristics often had to be inferred from the description as well. Objects that were apparently not left rough were coded as 2 (smooth) rather than 3 (polished) unless it was specifically stated that the object was polished or that a great amount of time was spent working on the object's surface.

SIZE. Size was often inferred from the description. Personal ornaments such as pendants or earrings were coded as 1 (small), unless a larger size was specifically given. Strings of shell beads were coded as 2 (medium) unless it was stated that they could be broken down into small strings or single beads, in which case they would be coded as 4 (small or medium).

ACQ. Acquisition labor was generally guessed at from the nature of the raw materials needed for the object and my own ideas on how difficult it would be to acquire them. If an object were traded from foreigners, it was coded as having a high (3) acquisition labor.

MAN. Manufacturing labor was generally guessed at from my own ideas on how difficult it would be to make the object. European trade goods were coded as having a high (3) manufacturing labor.

DUR. Durability was generally guessed at from my own ideas on how long it would take for an object to degrade or be broken.

APP. Appearance was coded within these guidelines: raw materials were coded as 1 (natural); goods that were plain, without much color, design, or workmanship were coded as 2 (ordinary); goods with a lot of color, particularly bright color, intricate design or workmanship were coded as 3 (extraordinary); and goods with much bright color, complicated and detailed design, or extensive workmanship were coded as 4 (extravagant). Objects of gold, silver, and copper were generally coded as 3 (extraordinary).

SEXRES,AGERES,SOCRES,RITRES. Restrictions on the object's possession or use were only coded if they were specifically mentioned. If a society had few restrictions on the use of goods, then it was assumed that there would not be any on other goods, and they would be coded as 1 (none) for these variables. If there were some restrictions on the use of goods in a society, then other goods would be coded as 9 (unknown) for these variables.

EXCH. An object was considered to be exchanged if it were used in any sort of social payment, including brideprice, funerary distributions, and the like. The frequency of exchange was coded by my own understanding of how often events which used these goods took place.

FOR. The goods an object was exchanged for were only coded if mentioned specifically. In cases where a good was used for brideprice or entry into a ritual grade or the like, the good was coded as being exchanged for 8 (other/combination).

COST. Cost was coded only if specifically mentioned. In the case of brideprice and the like, the good was coded as 8 (no basis for comparison).

WHO. If the good moved freely in a stratified society, it was coded as 1 (no pattern). If it moved freely in an egalitarian society it was coded as 4 (same level). Otherwise the good was coded only as specifically mentioned.

REL. If a good moved freely both within a society and with foreigners, it was coded as 1 (no pattern). Otherwise it was only coded as specifically mentioned.

CHAR. Social characteristics were coded only if specifically mentioned. If a good were used as a standard of value or exchange, it was coded as 1 (none).

POW, TAB, PUN, DES. These were all coded similarly. If specific mention was made of an object having power, taboos, or the like, then these were coded. Otherwise the good was assumed to be similar to other goods in the society. If other goods had no taboos, were not destroyed, or the like, then it was assumed that the good being coded was similar, and would be coded as 1 (none or never). If other goods did have power, taboos, or the like, then the good being coded would be coded as 9 (unknown).

WHE. Personal ornaments and weapons were coded as being found in 1 (no specific area). Otherwise goods were coded as specifically mentioned.

DIS. Disposal refers to disposal in contexts other than graves. It was assumed that objects were not disposed of deliberately (1) unless other objects in the society were.

GRA. If goods were ordinarily placed in the grave of people then goods would be coded as 2 (sometimes) even if they were not specifically mentioned as being buried. Goods specifically mentioned in societies where goods were ordinarily placed in graves were coded as 3 (often). Goods were coded as 4 (always) only if it was specifically stated that they were always placed in graves.

Appendix B:
Brief Descriptions of Societies
Included in the Prestige-Goods Study

4-Lozi (HRAF #FQ 9)

A kingdom located on the floodplain of the Upper Zambezi River, based on agriculture, animal husbandry, and fishing. Political control was centralized in the king, who, in theory, controlled all land and products, but in practice could not refuse to let subjects use the land and produce. The king was supported by tribute, but was expected to give most of it back to the people. A hierarchy of lower-order chiefs stood between local villages and the king. The king was entitled to use certain emblems which are not described in detail in the literature. Goods restricted to the king included an eland-tail fly-switch, spears, a fertility pole, a magic horn, and a national drum. These items were apparently destroyed or buried with the king upon his death, and the burial areas of kings are greatly revered as being places of great power. Other political offices have similar types of symbols associated with them. The king also controlled foreign trade to some extent, and a common gift for the king to give a lesser chief was calico cloth, which that individual could apparently not have gotten otherwise. Goods coded for the kingdom of Lozi are numbers 0063 to 0072.

5-Mbundu (HRAF #FP 13)

A kingdom in central Angola, based upon agriculture, husbandry, hunting, and fishing. A series of political offices stood between the king and the people, the lowest order being the village headman, usually the head of a localized lineage. Bridewealth payments were important elements of social prestige, and although cattle formed the bulk of these, other objects, particularly shell beads traded from the north, were important. Shell ornaments were used to display wealth and social status. Goods coded for the Mbundu kingdom are numbers 0073 to 0077.

33-Kafa (Huntingford 1955)

A kingdom in Ethiopia, based on agriculture and animal husbandry. Political control was centralized in

the king, but with provincial and district chiefs acting as intermediaries between the common people and the king. The major item controlled by the king was gold. Only the king or someone with the king's permission was allowed to own or wear gold. Strict penalties would be incurred if one were to wear gold without permission. The king was also the only person who could wear the color green. Goods coded for the Kafa kingdom are numbers 0001 to 0022.

90-Tiwi (HRAF #OI 20; Hart, Pilling and Goodale 1988)

A big-man society in north Australia, based upon hunting, gathering, and fishing. Wealth was vital to political power and prestige, particularly as it allowed one to purchase wives, and through them, to have daughters that could be "sold" to others. There were no particular items of wealth; all objects showing great craftsmanship were considered valuable. The only good coded for the Tiwi is number 0132.

97-New Ireland (HRAF #OM 10)

A big-man society in Melanesia, based on horticulture and fishing. Wealth in shell "money" was an important element of prestige and power. One of the most advantageous ways for an individual to increase their prestige was to sponsor a funerary feast, or *malangon*, for a dead relative. Paying a large bride-price for one's (or a relative's) wife also increased prestige. There were two forms of shell money in New Ireland, red and white. The red was considered to be of much greater value than white. Goods coded for New Ireland are numbers 0116 and 0117.

98-Trobriand Islanders (HRAF #OL 6)

A chiefdom in Melanesia, based upon horticulture and fishing. Chiefs had weak coercive power over people based upon their wealth and renown in Kula exchanges. Kula goods were shell arm-bands, decorated with ribbons of dried pandanus and shell beads, and shell necklaces made of flat round disks of red spondylus. Goods coded for the Trobriand Islanders are numbers 0055 and 0056.

99-Suiai (Oliver 1955)

A big-man society on Bouganville Island to the east of New Guinea, based upon horticulture, animal husbandry, and fishing. Big-men's power was based in part on their control of both pigs and shell "money." Shell money was also important in making bridewealth and funerary payments. Goods coded for Suiai are numbers 0035 to 0037.

102-Fiji (Williams 1884; Thompson 1940)

A chiefdom in extreme eastern Melanesia, based upon horticulture and fishing. The chief had great power, although elders in various districts could apparently counter the chief's power and held considerable power locally as well. Power and prestige could be gained through a competitive form of ceremonial gift exchange called *solevu*. Whale's teeth were the most valuable item of exchange, but pandanus mats and fine barkcloth were also important. Chiefs were given these valuables as tribute, as well as first-fruits. The wearing of a white turban was restricted to certain people of high rank. The chiefs and some priests were apparently the only ones allowed to wear red feathers. The goods coded for Fiji are numbers 0023 to 0029.

103-Ajie (Leenhardt 1930)

A chiefdom in southern Melanesia, based upon horticulture and fishing. Chiefs had some symbols of rank, including ritual hatchets. The most important wealth object was shell "money," darker forms of shell being valued the most. Shell money was used in a variety of social contexts, including bridewealth, funerary, peace, and other social payments. Generosity and giving away of wealth were important sources of prestige and political power, particularly during the ritual occasion of *pilou pilou*. Goods coded for the Ajie are numbers 0043 to 0046.

104-Maori (HRAF #OZ 4)

A chiefdom in New Zealand, based upon horticulture and fishing. Although the title of chief was inherited, an individual also needed to be wealthy in order to maintain power: "The prestige of a chief was bound up with his free use of wealth." Wealth had to flow through the chief's hands to others, so his prestige was based more on his generosity than on his direct wealth. Wealth itself was not measured by any standard of value, but by an object's age and decoration: "objects of superutility, with their artistic finish and extra need of labor embodied in their execution, commonly acquire especial value." There were,

however, some goods, such as greenstone, whale's teeth, and shark's teeth, that were considered valuable in and of themselves. Goods coded for the Maori are numbers 0118 to 0122.

105-Marquesans (HRAF #OX 6)

A chiefdom in eastern Polynesia, based upon horticulture, husbandry, and fishing. The Marquesans present somewhat of a problem. While they appear to be part of an obvious prestige-good system, the goods used are not well-described. Political power and prestige are strongly associated with wealth: "it appears that a chief arrived at his position of authority through social prestige and power resultant upon being the head of a large and wealthy family;" "Families were constantly trying to raise their status, which could be done only by accumulating and dispensing wealth." Wealth was also necessary for some social occasions. Marriages between high-status families apparently were preceeded by gifts, but what constituted these gifts is not discussed in any of the HRAF sources. Tattooing also required a young man to ally himself with a wealthy individual, for it was apparently very expensive to be tattooed. Again, the form of the expense is unfortunately not well described. Barkcloth and whale's teeth were mentioned in a few of the texts, but without direct reference to social payments or gifts. It can probably be assumed that they were prestige-goods, although there was not enough evidence to warrant their being coded. Indeed, no goods were coded for the Marquesan chiefdom.

106-Samoans (HRAF #OU 8)

A chiefdom in Polynesia based upon horticulture and fishing. In this markedly stratified society, power and prestige could be gained by the acquisition and distribution of wealth: "the Samoan gained prestige and authority through his generosity in distributing rather than his sagacity in accumulating wealth." Two of the most important wealth items were fine pandanus mats and bark cloth. Both formed a medium of exchange by which other goods could be valued. Goods coded for the Samoan chiefdom are numbers 0106 and 0107.

113-Atayal (LeBar 1975, Mabuchi 1960)

A headmanship in Formosa, based upon horticulture, hunting, and fishing. Strings of shell beads were used as a standard of exchange, as well as for brideprice and punitive damages. Weaving was considered an important skill for women, and finely woven hemp cloth was greatly valued. There was an elaborate system of graded insignia for marking social status or office, but these are not well described. Goods coded for the Atayal are numbers 0084 to 0088.

122-Ingalik (Osgood 1940)

A chiefdom in western Alaska, based upon hunting and fishing. Chiefs owed their power in part to their generosity and wealth. Skins, red ochre (for men), and dentalium shells (for women) were important wealth items. These were often distributed by chiefs at potlatch-like events. Goods coded for the Ingalik are numbers 0038 to 0042.

130-Eyak (Birket-Smith and de Laguna 1938)

A chiefdom in Alaska, based on hunting and fishing. Chiefs were hereditary, but maintained their positions through their wealth and generosity, mainly shown at potlatches. Important wealth items included blankets and furs. These items were also used to pay social debts, particularly punitive damages for murder. Goods coded for the Eyak are numbers 0054 and 0055.

131-Haida (Murdock 1934; Goddard 1934)

A chiefdom on the northwest coast of North America, based upon hunting and fishing. The chief occupied an hereditary position in a local lineage, but his power was based in large measure upon his ability give away wealth ceremonially at a potlatch. Important wealth items included furs, trade blankets, and decorated sheets of copper. Chiefs also had exclusive use of particular design emblems associated with their position. Goods coded for the Haida are numbers 0030 to 0034.

133-Twana (Elmendorf 1960)

A chiefdom in the northwestern United States, based upon hunting and fishing. Political power was based in large measure upon wealth and generosity. The most important wealth objects were strings of dentalium shells, wool blankets of either native (dog or mountain-goat fur) or European manufacture, and certain furs, particularly sea-otter. Generosity was occasioned at funerary potlatches (particularly those of dead political leaders, with aspiring leaders trying to show their wealth and generosity in order to assume the deceased's position), and through bridewealth and other social payments. Goods coded for the Twana are numbers 0050 to 0052.

134-Yurok (HRAF #NS 31)

A chiefdom in the northwestern United States, based upon hunting and fishing. The pursuit of wealth was a passion for the Yurok, and wealth brought with it prestige and power: "[chiefs] are individuals whose wealth, and their ability to retain and employ it, have clustered about them an aggregation of kinsmen, followers, and semidependents to whom they dispense assistance and protection." The major wealth items were dentalium shell "money," wood-pecker scalps, and obsidian blades. These items were used in brideprice payments and other exchanges, and funerary payments if a relative died away from home. Goods coded for the Yurok chiefdom are numbers 0108 to 0112.

135-Pomo (HRAF #NS 18)

A chiefdom in California, based upon hunting, fishing, and gathering. Although some chiefs held hereditary positions, "What may be termed an honorary captainship was accorded any man who, through his wealth...made himself very popular by providing large quantities of food and numerous feasts for the people." Objects that were considered valuable to the Pomo included shell discs and magnetite cylinder beads. Both were used in brideprice and funerary distributions, and as gifts following girls' puberty rites. Goods coded for the Pomo are numbers 0113 to 0115.

138-Klamath (HRAF #NR 10)

A chiefdom in the northwestern United States, based upon hunting and fishing. Although social status and political position could be inherited, wealth was an important element of political power. Its most important use was in the payment of brideprice, which had to be extravagant if one wanted to show oneself to be of high status. Items of value included dentalium and other types of shell beads, furs and hides, blankets, and Plains-type clothing. Goods coded for the Klamath are numbers 0057 to 0062.

143-Omaha (HRAF #NQ 12)

A chiefdom in the western United States, based on horticulture and hunting. Although some political positions and privileges were inherited, political power and social prestige could also be bought. A series of ranked offices existed that could be purchased with a variety of particular items, such as eagle war bonnets, catlinite pipes with decorated stems, ornamented tobacco pouches, and the like. Some of these items were also used to pay brideprice and shamans. Goods coded for the Omaha chiefdom are numbers 0123 to 0131.

144-Huron (Tooker 1964, Trigger 1969)

A chiefdom in the northeastern United States, based upon horticulture and hunting. Chiefly power was partly inherited, but "chiefs profited from the control of...[trade] routes and were well provided with trade goods that they could distribute among their followers to validate and enhance their status." Among the goods used to enhance status, and also for marriage and funerary payments, were strings of shell beads (wampum) and certain furs (black squirrel and beaver).

Chiefs also had "council sticks," which may have served as mnemonic or tallying devices, as well as other emblems of office that were not described in detail. Goods coded for the Hurons are numbers 0047 to 0049.

145-Creek (HRAF #NN 11)

A chiefdom in the southeastern United States, based upon horticulture and hunting. The chief was considered divine, but had little coercive control over the people. Most decisions were made by agreement of a local council. The chief did extract tribute and lead religious ceremonies. The color white was apparently the emblem of civil rule, while red was the emblem of military rule. Strings of shell beads or trade beads were used as a standard of exchange. The goods coded for the Creek chiefdom are numbers 0089 to 0091.

148-Apache (HRAF #NT 8)

A headmanship in the western United States based upon hunting and gathering. Political power and prestige were related to wealth: "The tie between leadership and wealth is a close one...." A wealthy individual was also expected to be generous. Abalone and turquoise were considered valuable, but there was no standard value for measuring wealth. Wealthy individuals did have certain kinds of clothing, such as high-topped moccasins. Goods coded for the Apache are numbers 0094 to 0099.

157-Bribri (HRAF #SA 19)

A headmanship in Costa Rica based on horticulture and fishing. Exchange with surrounding peoples was an important activity for the Bribri, and wealth was directly associated with prestige. There was apparently a form of brideprice among the Bribri, paid in trade cloth. Individuals were buried with all their valuables. Goods coded for the Bribri are numbers 0078 to 0083.

167-Cubeo (Goldman 1966)

A headmanship in Columbia based upon fishing, hunting, and horticulture. Political power and prestige were based largely upon wealth and generosity. There were a number of insignia for the highest ranking lineages (which are generally the most wealthy as well), such as silver necklaces and quartz pendants. The most important prestige items were feathers used in a feathered ceremonial headdress. Only the most prestigious had a full set of these feathers, because they were considered powerful and dangerous if one could not control them. Goods coded for the Cubeo are numbers 0100 to 0105.

172-Aymara (HRAF #SF 5)

A headmanship in Bolivia, based on horticulture and husbandry. Wealth was the major source of political power and prestige: "wealth is, with few exceptions, a necessary prerequisite to prestige and high status in the community." There was, however, no formal standard of wealth. Wealth was measured by one's home, their clothing, and their possessions. Generosity with one's wealth was an important avenue to prestige, particularly through the sponsorship of feasts. Goods coded for the Aymara are numbers 0092 and 0093.

Bibliography

Birket-Smith, Kaj and Frederica de Laguna
  1938 *The Eyak Indians of the Copper River Delta, Alaska.* Levin and Munksgaard, Copenhagen.
Elmendorf, William
  1960 *The Structure of Twana Culture.* Washington State University Research Studies 8(3), Monographic Supplement, Number 2. Pullman.
Goddard, Pliny Earle
  1972 *Indians of the Northwest Coast.* Cooper Square, New York.
Goldman, Irving
  1966 *The Cubeo.* Illinois Studies in Anthropology, Number 2. Urbana.
Hart, C.W.M., Arnold Pilling, and Jane Goodale
  1988 *The Tiwi of North Australia, 3rd Edition.* Holt, Rinehart and Winston, New York.
Huntingford, George W.B.
  1955 *The Galla of Ethiopia: the Kingdoms of Kafa and Janjero.* International African Institute, London.
LeBar, Frank
  1975 *Ethnic Groups in Insular Southeast Asia, Volume 2: Phillipines and Formosa.* HRAF, New Haven.
Leenhardt, Maurice
  1930 *Notes d'Ethnologie Neo-Caledonienne.* Travaux et Memoires de l'Institut d'Ethnologie, Paris, 8.

Mabuchi, Toichi
   1960 The Aboriginal Peoples of Formosa. *Viking Fund Publications in Anthropology,* Number 29:127-140.
Murdock, George P.
   1934 *Our Primitive Contemporaries.* MacMillian, New York.
Oliver, Douglas
   1955 *A Solomon Island Society.* Harvard, Cambridge, Massachusetts.
Osgood, Cornelius
   1940 *Ingalik Material Culture.* Yale University Publications in Anthropology 22. New Haven.
Thompson, Laura
   1940 *Southern Lau, Fiji: An Ethnography.* Bernice P. Bishop Museum Bulletin 162. Honolulu.
Tooker, Elizabeth
   1964 *An Ethnography of the Huron Indians, 1615-1649.* Bureau of American Ethnology Bulletin 190. Washington, D.C.
Trigger, Bruce G.
   1969 *The Huron: Farmers of the North.* Holt, Rinehart and Winston, New York.
Williams, Thomas
   1884 *Fiji and the Fijians.* Hodder and Stoughton, London.

Appendix C:
Codebook for Mississippian Burial Study

Cols.	Var.	Description			
1-3	CASE	Case number			
4-5	SITE	Site number			
		1-Yokem	2-Schild	3-Stone Quarry	
		4-DeFrenne	5-Mitchell	10-Toqua	11-Martin Farm
6	SEX	Sex			
		1-male	2-female	9-unknown	
7	AGE	Age			
		1-infant	2-juvenile	3-adult	4-senile
		9-unknown			
SHELL ARTIFACTS					
9-12	SSBEAD	Number of small shell beads			
13-14	LSBEAD	Number of large shell beads			
15-16	SPIN	Nnumber of shell pins			
17-18	SPEN	Number of shell pendants			
19-20	SGOR	Number of shell gorgets			
21-22	SMASK	Number of shell masks			
23-24	SPLUG	Number of shell ear/lip plugs			
25-26	SCUP	Number of engraved shell cups			
27-28	SCOL	Number of columella			
29-31	SPER	Number of pearl beads			
32-33	SUN	Number of unidentified shell ornaments			
34-35	SWORK	Number of unidentified worked shell pieces			
COPPER ARTIFACTS					
37-39	CBEAD	Number of copper beads			
40-41	CPEN	Number of copper pendants			
42-43	CGOR	Number of copper gorgets			
44-45	CPLUG	Number of copper lip plugs/ear spools			
46-47	CHAIR	Number of copper hair ornaments			
48-49	CROLL	Number of copper rolls/sheets			
50-51	CCOV	Number of copper-covered ornaments			
52-53	CUN	Number of unidentified copper ornaments			
54-55	CWORK	Number of unidentified worked copper pieces			

Continued

Cols.	Var.	Description
MINERAL ARTIFACTS		
57-58	MRMICA	Pieces of raw mica
59-60	MWMICA	Pieces of worked mica
61-62	MRGAL	Pieces of raw galena
63-64	MWGAL	Pieces of worked galena
65-66	MOCH	Pieces of red ochre
67-68	MGRAPH	Pieces of graphite
69-70	MROTH	Pieces of other raw minerals
71-72	MWOTH	Pieces of other worked minerals
73-74	MQBEAD	Number of quartzite beads
75-76	MQPEN	Number of quartzite pendants
77-78	MQOTH	Number of other quartzite ornaments
CARD TWO		
1-3	CASE2	Case number
STONE ARTIFACTS		
5-8	STBEAD	Number of stone beads
9-10	STPEN	Number of stone pendants
11-12	STGOR	Number of stone gorgents
13-14	STPLUG	Number of stone ear/lip plugs
15-16	STOTH	Number of other ornaments
17-18	STUN	Number of unidentified stone ornaments
19-20	STCELT	Number of ceremonial celts
21-22	STAXE	Number of ceremonial axes
23-24	STCER	Number of other ceremonial stone goods
BONE ARTIFACTS		
26-27	BBEADS	Number of bone beads
28-29	BPEN	Number of bone pendants
30-31	BGOR	Number of bone gorgets
32-33	BPLUG	Number of bone ear/lip plugs
34-35	BPIN	Number of bone pins
36-37	BOTH	Number of other bone ornaments
38-39	BUN	Number of unidentified bone ornaments

References Cited

Abu-Lughod, Janet
　1989　*Before European Hegemony: The World-System A.D. 1250-1350.* Oxford University Press, New York.
Anderberg, Michael
　1973　*Cluster Analysis for Applications.* Academic Press, New York.
Bach, Robert L.
　1980　On the Holism of a World-Systems Perspective. In *Processes of the World-System,* edited by T.K. Hopkins and I. Wallerstein, pp. 289-318. Sage, Beverly Hills, California.
Bender, Barbara
　1985a　Emergent Tribal Formations in the American Midcontinent. *American Antiquity* 50(1):52-62.
　1985b　Prehistoric Developments in the American Midcontinent and in Brittany, Northwest France. In *Prehistoric Hunter-Gatherers: The Emergence of Cultural Complexity,* edited by T.D. Price and J.A. Brown, pp. 21-58. Academic Press, New York.
Berg, Howard
　1983　*Random Walks in Biology.* Princeton University Press, Princeton, New Jersey.
Blanton, Richard
　n.d.　The Aztec Market System and the Growth of Empire. Ms. in possession of author.
　1987　A Comparative Political Economy of Empires. Paper presented at the American Anthropological Association meetings, Chicago.
Blanton, Richard and Gary Feinman
　1984　The Mesoamerican World-System. *American Anthropologist* 86(3):673-682.
Blanton, Richard, S. Kowalewski, G. Feinman, J. Appel
　1981　*Ancient Mesoamerica.* Cambridge University Press, New York.
Boas, Franz
　1966　*Kwakiutl Ethnography,* edited by H. Codere. University of Chicago Press, Chicago.
Brain, Jeffrey
　1978　Late Prehistoric Settlement Patterning in the Yazoo Basin and Natchez Bluffs Regions of the Lower Mississippi Valley. In *Mississippian Settlement Patterns,* edited by B.D. Smith, pp. 331-368. Academic Press, New York.
Braun, David and Stephen Plog
　1983　Evolution of "Tribal" Social Networks: Theory and Prehistoric North American Evidence. *American Antiquity* 47(3):504-525
Brose, David
　1978　Late Prehistory of the Upper Great Lakes Area. In *Northeast,* edited by B.G. Trigger, pp. 569-582. Handbook of North American Indians, vol. 15, W.G. Sturtevant, general editor. Smithsonian Institution, Washington, D.C.
　1979　A Speculative Model of the Role of Exchange in the Prehistory of the Eastern Woodlands. In *Hopewell Archaeology,* edited by D. Brose and N. Greber, pp. 3-8. Kent State University Press, Kent, Ohio.
Brose, David, James Brown and David Penney
　1985　*Ancient Art of the American Woodland Indians.* Harry N. Abrams, New York.
Brown, James (editor)
　1971　*Approaches to the Social Dimensions of Mortuary Practices.* Memoirs of the Society for American Archaeology No. 25. Washington, D.C.

Brown, James, Robert Bell and Don Wyckoff
1978 Caddoan Settlement Patterns in the Arkansas River Drainage. In *Mississippian Settlement Patterns*, edited by B.D. Smith, pp. 169-200. Academic Press, New York.

Brown, James, Richard Kerber and Howard Winters
1990 Trade and the Evolution of Exchange Relations at the Beginning of the Mississippian Period. In *The Mississippian Emergence*, edited by B.D. Smith, pp. 251-280. Smithsonian Institution, Washington, D.C.

Brunton, Ron
1975 Why do the Trobriands have Chiefs? *Man* 10:544-58.

Buikstra, Jane
1976 *Hopewell in the Lower Illinois River Valley*. Northwestern University Archaeological Program Scientific Papers No. 2. Evanston, Illinois.
1977 Biocultural Dimensions of Archaeological Study: A Regional Perspective. In *Biocultural Adaptation in Prehistoric America*, edited by R. Blakely, pp. 67-84. University of Georgia Press, Athens.

Buikstra, Jane, Lyle Konigsberg and Jull Bullington
1986 Fertility and the Development of Agriculture in the Prehistoric Midwest. *American Antiquity* 51(3):528-546.

Buikstra, Jane, J. Bullington, D. Charles, D. Cook, S. Frankenberg, L. Konigsberg, J. Lambert and L Xue
1987 Diet, Demography, and the Development of Agriculture. In *Emergent Horticultural Economies of the Eastern Woodlands*, edited by W. Keegan, pp. 67-86. Center for Archaeological Investigations Occasional Papers No. 7. Southern Illinois University, Carbondale.

Cadillac, Antoine de la Mothe
1962 Memoir of LaMothe Cadillac [1692]. In *The Western Country in the 17th Century*, edited by M.M. Quaife, pp. 3-83. Citadel Press, New York.

Caldwell, Joseph
1958 *Trend and Tradition in the Prehistory of the Eastern United States*. American Anthropological Association Memoir 88. Washington, D.C.

Chapman, Jefferson
1985 *Tellico Archaeology*. Tennessee Valley Authority Publications in Anthropology No. 41. Knoxville, Tennessee.

Chapman, Robert, Ian Kinnes and Klavs Randsborg
1981 *The Archaeology of Death*. Cambridge University Press, New York.

Charles, Douglas and Jane Buikstra
1983 Archaic Mortuary Sites in the Central Mississippi Drainage: Distribution, Structure, and Behavioral Implications. In *Archaic Hunters and Gatherers in the American Midwest*, edited by J. Phillips and J. Brown, pp.117-146. Academic Press, New York.

Chase-Dunn, Christopher and Thomas Hall (editors)
1991a *Core/Periphery Relations in Precapitalist Worlds*. Westview Press, Boulder.

Chase-Dunn, Christopher and Thomas Hall
1991b Conceptualizing Core/Periphery Hierarchies for Comparative Study. In *Core/Periphery Relations in Precapitalist Worlds*, edited by C. Chase-Dunn and T. Hall, pp. 1-44. Westview Press, Boulder.

Chmurny, William
1973 *The Ecology of the Middle Mississippian Occupation of the American Bottom*. Ph.D. Dissertation, Department of Anthropology, University of Illinois, Urbana. University Microfilms, Ann Arbor.

Clark, Grahame
1986 *Symbols of Excellence: Precious Materials as Expression of Status*. Cambridge University Press, London.

Codere, Helen
1950 *Fighting with Property*. Monographs of the American Ethological Society No. 20. J.J. Augustin, New York.

Cook, K.S., R.M. Emerson, M.R. Gilmore and T. Yamagishi
1983 The Distribution of Power in Exchange Networks: Theory and Experimental Results. *American Journal of Sociology* 89(2):275-305.

Cruz, Joan
    1984 *Relics*. Our Sunday Visitor, Huntington, Indiana.
Curtis, Edward
    1915 *The Kwakiutl*. The North American Indian, vol. 10. Published privately by Edward S. Curtis.
Davidson, Janet
    1979 Samoa and Tonga. In *The Prehistory of Polynesia*, edited by J. Jennings, pp. 82-109. Harvard University Press, Cambridge, Massachusetts.
DeLiette, Louis (DeGannes)
    1934 Memoir of DeGannes Concerning the Illinois Country [1702]. In *Collections of the Illinois State Historical Library*, vol. 23, edited by T.C. Pease, pp. 302-395. Springfield, Illinois.
DePratter, Chester
    1983 *Late Prehistoric and Early Historic Chiefdoms in the Southeastern United States*. Ph.D. Dissertation, Department of Anthropology, University of Georgia, Athens. University Microfilms, Ann Arbor.
Dincauze, Dina and Robert Hasenstab
    1989 Explaining the Iroquois: Tribalization on a Prehistoric Periphery. In *Centre and Periphery*, edited by T. Champion, pp. 67-84. Unwin Hyman, London.
Drennan, Robert
    1987 Regional Demography in Chiefdoms. In *Chiefdoms in the Americas*, edited by R.D. Drennan and C.A. Uribe, pp. 307-323. University Press of America, Lantham, Massachusetts.
Droessler, Judith
    1981 *Craniometry and Biological Distance*. Center for American Archaeology, Evanston, Illinois.
Earle, Timothy
    1987 Chiefdoms in an Archaeological and Ethnohistorical Perspective. *Annual Review of Anthropology* 16:279-308.
Ekholm, Kajsa
    1972 *Power and Prestige: The Rise and Fall of the Kongo Kingdom*. Scriv Service, Uppsala, Netherlands.
    1977 External Exchange and the Transformation of Central African Social Systems. In *The Evolution of Social Systems*, edited by J. Friedman and M.J. Rowlands, pp. 115-136. Duckworth, London.
Errington, Frederick
    1974 *Karavar: Masks and Power in a Melanesian Ritual*. Cornell University Press, Ithaca, New York.
Errington, Shelly
    1977 Order and Power in Karavar. In *The Anthropology of Power*, edited by R.D. Fogelson and R.N. Adams, pp. 23-43. Academic Press, New York.
Essenpreis, Patricia
    1978 Fort Ancient Settlement: Differential Response at a Mississippian-Late Woodland Interface. In *Mississippian Settlement Patterns*, edited by B.D. Smith, pp. 141-168. Academic Press, New York.
Everitt, Brian
    1974 *Cluster Analysis*. John Wiley & Sons, New York.
Feinman, Gary and Jill Neitzel
    1984 Too Many Types: An Overview of Sedentary Prestate Societies in the Americas. In *Advances in Archaeological Method and Theory*, vol. 7, edited by M. Schiffer, pp. 9-102. Academic Press, New York.
Feinman, Gary and Linda Nicholas
    1991 The Monte Alban State: A Diachronic Perspective on an Ancient Core and its Periphery. In *Core/Periphery Relations in Precapitalist Worlds*, edited by C. Chase-Dunn and T. Hall, pp. 240-276. Westview Press, Boulder.
Ferdon, Edwin
    1987 *Early Tonga*. University of Arizona Press, Tuscon.
Ford, Richard
    1974 Northeastern Archaeology: Past and Future Directions. *Annual Review of Anthropology* 3:385-413.
    1977 Evolutionary Ecology and the Evolution of Human Ecosystems: A Case Study from the Midwestern U.S.A. In *Explanation of Prehistoric Change*, edited by J.W. Hill, pp. 153-184. University of New Mexico Press, Albuquerque.

Fowler, Melvin
    1974 *Cahokia: Ancient Capital of the Midwest.* Addison-Wesley Module in Anthropology No. 48. Reading, Massachusetts.
    1977 The Cahokia Site. In *Explorations into Cahokia Archaeology*, edited by M. Fowler, pp. 1-30. Illinois Archaeological Survey Bulletin No. 7, Second Revised Edition. University of Illinois, Urbana.
    1978 Cahokia and the American Bottom: Settlement Archaeology. In *Mississippian Settlement Patterns*, edited by B.D. Smith, pp. 455-478. Academic Press, New York.

Fowler, Melvin and Robert Hall
    1978 Late Prehistory of the Illinois Area. In *Northeast*, edited by B.G. Trigger, pp. 560-568. Handbook of North American Indians, vol. 15, W. Sturtevant, general editor. Smithsonian Institution, Washington, D.C..

Frankenstein, Susan and Michael Rowlands
    1978 The Internal Structure and Regional Context of Early Iron Age Society in South-Western Germany. *Bulletin of the Institute of Archaeology of London* 15:73-112.

Freeman, Linton
    1979 Centrality in Social Networks I: Conceptual Clarification. *Social Networks* 1:215-239.

Friedman, Johnathan
    1982 Catastrophe and Continuity in Social Evolution. In *Theory and Explanation in Archaeology*, edited by C. Renfrew, M.J. Rowlands, and B.A. Segraves, pp. 175-196. Academic Press, New York.

Friedman, Johnathan and Michael Rowlands
    1977 Notes Towards an Epigenetic Model of the Evolution of "Civilisation." In *The Evolution of Social Systems*, edited by J. Friedman and M. Rowlands, pp. 201-275. Duckworth, London.

Fry, Robert
    1979 The Economics of Pottery at Tikal, Guatemala: Models of Exchange for Serving Vessels. *American Antiquity* 44(3):494-512.

Galloway, Patricia (editor)
    1989 *The Southeastern Ceremonial Complex.* University of Nebraska Press, Lincoln.

Geary, Patrick
    1978 *Furta Sacra: Thefts of Relics in the Central Middle Ages.* Princeton University Press, Princeton, New Jersey.

Gifford, E.W.
    1929 *Tongan Society.* Bernice P. Bishop Museum Bulletin No. 61. Honolulu.

Goad, Sharon
    1978 *Exchange Networks in the Prehistoric Southeastern United States.* Ph.D. Dissertation, Department of Anthropology, University of Georgia, Athens. University Microfilms, Ann Arbor.

Goldman, Irving
    1970 *Ancient Polynesian Society.* University of Chicago Press, Chicago.

Goldstein, Lynne
    1980 *Mississippian Mortuary Practices: A Case Study of Two Cemeteries in the Lower Illinois Valley.* Northwestern University Archaeology Program Scientific Papers No. 4. Evanston, Illinois.

Goodman, Claire G.
    1984 *Copper Artifacts in Late Eastern Woodlands Prehistory,* edited by A. Cantwell. Center for American Archeology, Evanston, Illinois.

Green, Thomas
    1977 *Economic Relationships Underlying Mississippian Settlement Patterns in Southeastern Indiana.* Ph.D. Dissertation, Department of Anthropology, Indiana University, Bloomington. University Microfilms, Ann Arbor.

Griffin, James (editor)
    1952 *Archaeology of Eastern United States.* University of Chicago Press, Chicago.

Griffin, James
    1967 Eastern North American Archaeology: A Summary. *Science* 156:175-191.
    1978a The Midlands and Northeastern United States. In *Ancient Native Americans*, edited by J. Jennings, pp. 221-280. W.H. Freeman, San Francisco.

1978b Late Prehistory of the Ohio Valley. In *Northeast*, edited by B.G. Trigger, pp. 547-559. Handbook of North American Indians, vol. 15, W. Sturtevant, general editor. Smithsonian Institution, Washington, D.C..

1985 Changing Concepts of the Prehistoric Mississippian Cultures of the Eastern United States. In *Alabama and the Borderlands*, edited by R.R. Badger and L.A. Clayton, pp. 40-63. University of Alabama Press, Tuscaloosa.

Hage, Per and Frank Harary
1983 *Structural Models in Anthropology*. Cambridge University Press, New York.

Haggett, Peter and Richard Chorley
1969 *Network Analysis in Geography*. St. Martin's Press, New York.

Haggett, Peter, Andrew Cliff and Allan Frey
1977 Locational Analysis in Human Geography, 2d ed. Edward Arnold, London.

Harary, Frank
1969 *Graph Theory*. Addison-Wesley, Reading, Massachusetts.

Harary, Frank, Robert Norman and Dorwin Cartwright
1965 *Structural Models: An Introduction to the Theory of Directed Graphs*. John Wiley & Sons, New York.

Harn, Alan
1978 Mississippian Settlement Patterns in the Central Illinois River Valley. In *Mississippian Settlement Patterns.*, edited by B.D. Smith, pp. 233-268. Academic Press, New York.

Hatch, James W.
1974 *Social Dimensions of Dallas Mortuary Practices*. Unpublished master's thesis, Department of Anthropology, Pennsylvania State University, University Park.

d'Haucourt, Genevieve
1963 *Life in the Middle Ages*. Walker and Co, New York.

Helmkamp, R. Criss
1985 *Biosocial Organization and Change in East Tennessee Late Woodland and Mississippian*. Ph.D. Dissertation, Department of Sociology and Anthropology, Purdue University, West Lafayette. University Microfilms, Ann Arbor.

Helms, Mary
1979 *Ancient Panama: Chiefs in Search of Power*. University of Texas Press, Austin.
1988 *Ulysses' Sail*. Cambridge University Press, New York.

Hilton, Anne
1985 *The Kingdom of Kongo*. Clarendon Press, Oxford.

Hodder, Ian (editor)
1982 *Symbols in Action: Ethnoarchaeological Studies of Material Culture*. Cambridge University Press, New York.

Hopkins, Terence K.
1982 World-Systems Analysis: Methodological Issues. In *World-Systems Analysis: Theory and Methodology*, edited by T.K. Hopkins and I. Wallerstein, pp. 145-158. Sage, Beverly Hills, California.

Hopkins, Terence, and Immanuel Wallerstein
1977 Patterns of World-System Development: A Research Proposal. *Review* 1(2):111-145.

Hudson, Charles
1976 *The Southeastern Indians*. University of Tennessee Press, Knoxville.

Irwin-Williams, Cynthia
1977 A Network Model for the Analysis of Prehistoric Trade. In *Exchange Systems in Prehistory*, edited by T.K. Earle and J.E. Ericson, pp. 141-151. Academic Press, New York.

Kaeppler, Adrienne
1971a Rank in Tonga. *Ethnology* 10(2):174-193.
1971b Eighteenth-Century Tonga: New Interpretations of Tongan Society and Material Culture at the Time of Captain Cook. *Man* 6(2):204-220.
1978 Exchange Patterns in Goods and Spouses: Fiji, Tonga and Samoa. *Mankind* 11(3):246-252.

Kelly, John
  1980 *Formative Developments at Cahokia and the Adjacent American Bottoms: A Merrell Tract Perspective.* Ph.D. Dissertation, Department of Anthropology, University of Wisconsin, Madison. University Microfilms, Ann Arbor.
Kinietz, Vernon
  1965 *Indians of the Western Great Lakes.* University of Michigan Press, Ann Arbor.
Kirch, Patrick
  1984 *The Evolution of the Polynesian Chiefdoms.* Cambridge University Press, New York.
Kneberg, Madeline
  1952 The Tennessee Area. In *Archaeology of Eastern United States*, edited by J.B. Griffin, pp. 190-198. University of Chicago Press, Chicago.
Lafferty, Robert
  1977 *The Evolution of Mississippian Settlement Patterns and Exploitative Technology in the Black Bottom of Southern Illinois.* Ph.D. Dissertation, Department of Anthropology, Southern Illinois University, Carbondale. University Microfilms, Ann Arbor.
Larson, Lewis
  1972 Functional Considerations of Warfare in the Southeast During the Mississippian Period. *American Antiquity* 37:383-392
Lewis, Thomas and Madeline Kneberg
  1946 *Hiwassee Island.* University of Tennessee Press, Knoxville.
Little, Elizabeth
  1987 Inland Waterways of the Northeast. *Midcontinental Journal of Archaeology* 12(1):55-76.
MacEvoy, Bruce and Linton Freeman
  1987 *UCINET: A Microcomputer Package for Network Analysis.* Mathematical Social Sciences Group, University of California, Irvine.
Maliowski, Bronislaw
  1920 Kula: The Circulating Exchanges of Valuables in the Archipelagoes of Eastern New Guinea. *Man* 51:97-105.
  1922 *Argonauts of the Western Pacific.* Routledge, London.
Mariner, William
  1817 *An Account of the Natives of the Tonga Islands*, edited by J. Martin. John Murray, London.
Markovsky, Barry, Travis Patton and David Willer
  1988 Power Relations in Exchange Networks. *American Sociological Review* 53:220-36.
Mason, Ronald
  1981 *Great Lakes Archaeology.* Academic Press, New York.
Meillassoux, Claude
  1978 "The Economy" in Agricultural Self-Sustaining Societies: A Preliminary Analysis. In *Relations of Production*, edited by D. Seddon, pp. 127-157. Frank Cass, London.
Milner, George R.
  1983 *The East St. Louis Stone Quarry Site Cemetery.* University of Illinois Press, Urbana.
  1984 Social and Temporal Implications of Variation Among American Bottom Mississippian Cemeteries. *American Antiquity* 49(3):468-488.
  1990 The Late Prehistoric Cahokia Cultural System of the Mississippi River Valley: Foundations, Florescence, and Fragmentation. *Journal of World Prehistory* 4(1):1-43.
Moorehead, Warren
  1923 *The Cahokia Mounds.* University of Illinois Bulletin No. 21. Urbana.
  1929 *The Cahokia Mounds.* University of Illinois Bulletin No. 26. Urbana.
Morse, Dan and Phyllis Morse
  1983 *Archaeology of the Central Mississippi Valley.* Academic Press, New York.
Muller, Jon
  1978 The Southeast. In *Ancient Native Americans*, edited by J. Jennings, pp. 281-326. W.H. Freeman, San Francisco.
  1986 *Archaeology of the Lower Ohio River Valley.* Academic Press, New York.
Murdock, George P. and Douglas R. White
  1969 The Standard Cross-Cultural Sample. *Ethnology* 8:329-369.

Myer, William
  1928 Indian Trails of the Southeast. In *42nd Annual Report of the Bureau of American Ethnology for the Years 1924-25*, pp.727-857. Washington, D.C.

Nag, Moni, Benjamin White and R.C. Peet
  1978 An Anthropological Approach to the Study of the Economic Value of Children in Java and Nepal. *Current Anthropology* 19(2):293-301.

Nieminen, U. Juhani
  1974 On the Centrality in a Graph. *Scandinavian Journal of Psychology* 15:332-336.

O'Brien, Patricia
  1989 Cahokia: The Political Capital of the "Ramey" State? *North American Archaeologist* 10(4):275-292.

Orr, Kenneth G.
  1951 Change at Kincaid: A Study of Cultural Dynamics. In *Kincaid*, edited by F. Cole, pp. 293-359. University of Chicago Press, Chicago.

Parker Pearson, Michael
  1982 Mortuary Practices, Society, and Ideology: An Ethnoarchaeological Study. In *Symbolic and Structural Archaeology*, edited by I. Hodder, pp. 99-114. Cambridge University Press, New York.

Patterson, Thomas
  1986 The Last Sixty Years: Toward a Social History of Americanist Archaeology in the United States. *American Anthropologist* 88(1):7-26.

Peebles, Christopher
  1978 Determinants of Settlement Size and Location in the Moundville Phase. In *Mississippian Settlement Patterns*, edited by B.D. Smith, pp. 369-416. Academic Press, New York.
  1987 The Rise and Fall of the Mississippian in Western Alabama: The Moundville and Summerville Phases, A.D. 1000 to 1600. *Mississippi Archaeology* 22(1):1-31.

Peebles, Christopher and Susan Kus
  1977 Some Archaeological Correlates of Ranked Society. *American Antiquity* 42:421-448.

Peregrine, Peter
  1987 *Miami-Jesuit Relations at Green Bay 1669-1679: A Study in Acculturation.* Unpublished master's thesis, Department of Sociology and Anthropology, Purdue University, West Lafayette.
  1988 The Political Economy of Jesuit Missioning in New France. Paper presented at the annual meeting of the American Society for Ethnohistory, Berkeley.
  1989a Indigenous World-Systems in Eastern America: An Introduction. Paper presented at the annual meeting of the American Society for Ethnohistory, Chicago.
  1989b World-Systems and Luxury Goods: A Rebuttal to Wallerstein. Paper presented at the annual meeting of the American Anthropological Association, Chicago.
  1990 *The Evolution of Mississippian Societies in the American Midcontinent from a World-System Perspective.* Ph.D. Dissertation, Department of Sociology and Anthropology, Purdue University, West Lafayette. University Microfilms, Ann Arbor.
  1991a Prehistoric Chiefdoms on the American Midcontinent: A World-System Based on Prestige-Goods. In *Core/Periphery Relations in Precapitalist Worlds*, edited by C. Chase-Dunn and T. Hall, pp. 193-211. Westview Press, Boulder.
  1991b Some Political Aspects of Craft Specialization. *World Archaeology* 23(1):1-11.
  1991c A Graph-Theoretic Approach to the Evolution of Cahokia. *American Antiquity* 56(1):66-75.

Perino, Gregory H.
  1971a The Yokem Site, Pike County, Illinois. In *Mississippian Site Archaeology in Illinois: I*, edited by J. Brown, pp. 149-186. Illinois Archaeological Survey Bulletin No. 8. University of Illinois, Urbana.
  1971b The Mississippian Component at the Schild Site, Greene County, Illinois. In *Mississippian Site Archaeology in Illinois: I*, edited by J. Brown, pp. 1-148. Illinois Archaeological Survey Bulletin No. 8. University of Illinois, Urbana.

Persson, John
  1983 Cyclical Change and Circular Exchange: A Re-examination of the Kula Ring. *Oceania* 54(1):32-47.

Phillips, Philip and James Brown
  1978 *Pre-Columbian Shell Engravings from the Craig Mound at Spiro, Oklahoma.* Paperback Edition, Part One. Peabody Museum Press, Cambridge, Massachusetts.

Piddocke, Stuart
   1969 The Potlatch System of the Southern Kwakiutl. In *Environment and Cultural Behavior*, edited by A.P. Vayda, pp. 130-156. University of Texas Press, Austin.
Pitts, Forrest
   1965 A Graph Theoretic Approach to Historical Geography. *The Professional Geographer* 17(5):15-20.
   1978 The Medieval River Trade Network of Russia Revisited. *Social Networks* 1:285-292.
Polhemus, Richard
   1987 *The Toqua Site - 40MR6: A Late Mississippian Dallas Phase Town*. Tennessee Valley Authority Publications in Anthropology No. 44. Knoxville, Tennessee.
Porter, James
   1974 *Cahokia Archaeology as Viewed from the Mitchell Site: A Satellite Community at A.D. 1150-1200*. Ph.D. Dissertation, Department of Anthropology, University of Wisconsin, Madison. University Microfilms, Ann Arbor.
Price, James
   1978 The Settlement Pattern of the Powers Phase. In *Mississippian Settlement Patterns*, edited by B.D. Smith, pp. 210-232. Academic Press, New York.
Raudot, Antoine Denis
   1965 Memoir Concerning the Different Indian Nations of North America. Translated by V. Kinietz. Appendix to *Indians of the Western Great Lakes*, by V. Kinitez, pp. 341-410. University of Michigan Press, Ann Arbor.
Reed, Nelson
   1977 Monks and Other Mississippian Mounds. In *Explorations into Cahokia Archaeology*, edited by M.L. Fowler, pp. 31-42. Illinois Archaeological Survey Bulletin No. 7, Second Revised Edition. University of Illinois, Urbana.
Renfrew, Colin
   1972 *The Emergence of Civilisation: The Cyclades and the Aegean in the Third Millenium BC*. Methuen, London.
   1975 Trade as Action at a Distance: Questions of Integration and Communication. In *Ancient Civilization and Trade*, edited by J. Sabloff and C.C. Lamberg-Karlovsky, pp. 3-59. University of New Mexico Press, Albuquerque.
   1977 Alternate Models for Exchange and Spatial Distribution. In *Exchange Systems in Prehistory*, edited by T.K. Earle and J.E. Ericson, pp. 71-90. Academic Press, New York.
   1982 Polity and Power: Interaction, Intensification and Exploitation. In *An Island Polity: The Archaeology of Exploitation in Melos*, edited by C. Renfrew and M. Wagstaff, pp. 264-290. Cambridge University Press, New York.
   1986 Introduction: Peer Polity Interaction and Socio-Political Change. In *Peer Polity Interaction and Socio-Political Change*, edited by C. Renfrew and J. Cherry, pp. 1-18. Cambridge University Press, New York.
Rothman, Mitchell S.
   1987 Graph Theory and the Interpretation of Regional Survey Data. *Paleorient* 13(2):73-91.
Rowlands, M.J., M. Larson and K. Kristiansen (editors)
   1987 *Centre and Periphery in the Ancient World*. Cambridge University Press, New York.
Rutherford, Noel (editor)
   1977 *Friendly Islands: A History of Tonga*. Oxford University Press, Oxford.
Sabidussi, Gert
   1966 The Centrality Index of a Graph. *Psychometrika* 31(4):581-603.
Salisbury, Richard
   1962 *From Stone to Steel*. Cambridge University Press, New York.
Schneider, Jane
   1977 Was There a "Pre-Capitalist" World-System? *Peasant Studies* 6(1):20-29.
Schroedl, Gerald, R.P.S. Davis, C.C. Boyd
   1985 *Archaeological Contexts and Assemblages at Martin Farm*. Tennessee Valley Authority Publications in Anthropology No. 37. Knoxville, Tennessee.

Sears, William
  1954 The Sociopolitical Organization of Pre-Columbian Cultures on the Gulf Coastal Plain. *American Anthropologist* 56:339-346.
Service, Elman
  1971 *Primitive Social Organization: An Evolutionary Perspective.* Random House, New York.
  1975 *Origins of the State and Civilization: The Process of Cultural Evolution.* W.W. Norton, New York.
Shanks, Michael and Christopher Tilley
  1987 *Social Theory and Archaeology.* University of New Mexico Press, Albuquerque.
Shils, Edward
  1971 Tradition. Comparative Studies in Society and History 13(2):122-59.
Smith, Bruce D.
  1978 Variation in Mississippian Settlement Patterns. In *Mississippian Settlement Patterns*, edited by B.D. Smith, pp. 479-504. Academic Press, New York.
  1984 Mississippian Expansion: Tracing the Historical Development of an Explanatory Model. *Southeastern Archaeology* 3(1):13-32.
  1987 Hopewellian Farmers of Eastern North America. Paper presented at the 11th Congress, International Union of Prehistoric and Protohistoric Sciences, Mainz, Germany.
Smith, Harriet
  1977 The Murdock Mound, Cahokia site. In *Explorations into Cahokia Archaeology*, edited by M. Fowler (ed.), pp. 49-88. Illinois Archaeological Survey Bulletin No. 7, Second Revised Edition. University of Illinois, Urbana.
Southern, Richard
  1970 *Western Society and the Church in the Middle Ages.* Pelican History of the Church, vol. 2. Wm. B. Eerdmans, Grand Rapids, Michigan.
Spaulding, Albert
  1955 Prehistoric Cultural Developments in the Eastern United States. In *New Interpretations of Aboriginal America Culture History*, pp. 12-27. Anthropological Society of Washington, Washington, D.C.
SPSS, Inc.
  1988 *SPSS-X User's Guide, Third Edition.* SPSS, Inc., Chicago.
Steponaitis, Vincas
  1986 Prehistoric Archaeology in the Southeastern United States, 1970-1985. *Annual Review of Anthropology* 15:363-404.
  1991 Contrasting Patterns of Mississippian Development. In *Chiefdoms: Power, Economy and Ideology*, edited by T. Earle, pp. 193-228. Cambridge University Press, New York.
Strathern, Andrew
  1971 *The Rope of Moka.* Cambridge University Press, New York.
Styles, Bonnie
  1981 *Faunal Exploitation and Resource Selection.* Northwestern University Archaeological Program Scientific Papers No. 3. Evanston, Illinois.
Taaffe, Edward and Howard Gauthier
  1973 *The Geography of Transportation.* Prentice-Hall, Engelwood Cliffs, New Jersey.
Tainter, J.A.
  1977a Woodland Social Change in West-Central Illinois. *Midcontinental Journal of Archaeology* 2(1):67-98.
  1977b Modeling Change in Prehistoric Social Systems. In *For Theory Building in Archaeology*, edited by L. Binford, pp. 327-351. Academic Press, New York.
  1978 Mortuary Practices and the Study of Prehistoric Social Systems. In *Advances in Archaeological Method and Theory*, vol. 1, edited by M. Schiffer, pp. 105-141. Academic Press, New York.
  1983 Woodland Social Change in the Central Midwest: A Review and Evaluation of Interpretive Trends. *North American Archaeologist* 4(2):141-161.
Thomas, Cyrus
  1985 *Report on the Mound Explorations of the Bureau of Ethnology.* Smithsonian Institution, Washington, D.C.

Thwaites, Reuben G. (editor)
 1896-1901 *The Jesuit Relations and Allied Documents*. 73 vols. Burrows Brothers, Cleveland.
Titterington, Paul
 1938 *The Cahokia Mound Group and its Village Site Materials*. P.F. Titterington, St Louis.
USGS (United States Geological Survey)
 1985 *National Water Summary 1985—Hydrologic Events and Surface-Water Resources*. USGS Water-Supply Paper 2300.
Vansina, Jan
 1966 *Kingdoms of the Savannah*. University of Wisconsin Press, Madison.
Wallerstien, Immanuel
 1974a *The Modern World-System, Volume 1*. Academic Press, New York.
 1974b The Rise and Future Demise of the Capitalist World-System: Concepts for Comparative Analysis. *Comparative Studies in Society and History* 16(4):387-415.
 1976 A World-System Perspective on the Social Sciences. *British Journal of Sociology* 27(3):343-352.
 1982 World-Systems Analysis: Theoretical and Interpretive Issues. In *World-Systems Analysis: Theory and Methodology*, edited by T.K. Hopkins and I. Wallerstein, pp. 91-103. Sage, Beverly Hills, California.
 1989 *The Modern World-System, Volume 3*. Academic Press, New York.
Ward, Trawick
 1965 Correlation of Mississippian Sites and Soil Types. *Southeastern Archaeololgical Conference Bulletin* 3:42-48.
Waring, A.J. and Preston Holder
 1945 A Prehistoric Ceremonial Complex in the Southeastern United States. *American Anthropologist* 47(1):1-34.
Weiner, Annette
 1976 *Women of Value, Men of Renown*. University of Texas Press, Austin.
 1989 *The Trobrianders of Papua New Guinea*. Holt, Rinehart and Winston, New York.
Welch, Paul A.
 1986 *Models of Chiefdom Economy: Prehistoric Moundville as a Case Study*. Ph.D. Dissertation, Department of Anthropology, University of Michigan, Ann Arbor. University Microfilms, Ann Arbor.
 1991 *Moundville's Economy*. University of Alabama Press, Tuscaloosa.
Willer, David
 1986 Vulnerability and the Location of Power Positions: Comment on Cook, Emerson, Gilmore, and Yamagishi. *American Journal of Sociology* 92(2):441-444.
Winters, Howard
 1968 Value Systems and Trade Cycles of the Late Archaic in the Midwest. In *New Perspectives in Archaeology*, edited by S.R. Binford and L.R. Binford, pp. 175-221. Aldine, Chicago.
Yamagishi, Toshio, Mary Gilmore and Karen Cook
 1988 Network Connections and the Distribution of Power in Exchange Networks. *American Journal of Sociology* 93(4):833-851.